Land Law
2010–2011

Routledge
Taylor & Francis Group

LONDON AND NEW YORK

Seventh edition published 2010
by Routledge
2 Park Square, Milton Park, Abingdon, Oxon OX14 4RN

Simultaneously published in the USA and Canada
by Routledge
270 Madison Avenue, New York, NY 10016

Routledge is an imprint of the Taylor & Francis Group, an informa business

© 2006, 2008, 2010 Routledge

Previous editions published by Cavendish Publishing Limited
First edition   1997
Second edition   1999
Third edition   2002
Fourth edition   2004

Typeset in Rotis by RefineCatch Limited, Bungay, Suffolk
Printed and bound in Great Britain by TJ International Ltd, Padstow, Cornwall

All rights reserved. No part of this book may be reprinted or
reproduced or utilised in any form or by any electronic,
mechanical, or other means, now known or hereafter
invented, including photocopying and recording, or in any
information storage or retrieval system, without permission in
writing from the publishers.

British Library Cataloguing in Publication Data
A catalogue record for this book is available from the British Library

Library of Congress Control Number: 2009912673

ISBN10: 0-415-56674-6 (pbk)
ISBN13: 978-0-415-56677-3 (pbk)

ISBN10: 0-203-85815-8 (eBook)
ISBN13: 978-0-203-85815-8 (eBook)

Contents

	Table of Cases	v
	Table of Statutes	xv
	Table of Statutory Instruments	xxiii
	Table of European Legislation	xxv
	Abbreviations	xxvii
	How to use this book	xxix
1	Fundamental concepts	1
2	Conveying title to land with unregistered title	11
3	Transferring title to land with registered title	19
4	Adverse possession and boundaries	31
5	Trusts of land	41
6	Resulting trusts, constructive trusts, proprietary estoppel and licences	55
7	Leases	67
8	Mortgages	85
9	Easements and *profits à prendre*	97
10	Freehold covenants	109
11	Putting it into practice . . .	121

Table of Cases

88 Berkeley Road, London NW9, Re [1983]	49
Abbey National Building Society v Cann [1991]	27
Abbey National plc v Moss [1994]	53
A G Securities v Vaughan [1990]	47, 77, 124
Alan Wibberley Building Ltd v Insley [1999]	38
Aldred's Case [1610]	100
Allen v Greenwood [1980]	101
Antoniades v Villiers [1992]	77
Ashburn Anstalt v Arnold [1989]	65, 74
Aslan v Murphy [1990]	77
Austerberry v Corporation of Oldham [1885]	114, 116
B & Q plc v Liverpool and Lancashire Properties Ltd [2001]	106
Bailey v Stephens [1862]	99
Baker v Baker [1993]	61
Banner v Luff Developments [2000]	10
Barca v Mears (2004)	54
Barclays Bank plc v O'Brien [1994]	91
Barnhart v Greenshields [1853]	7
Batchelor v Marlow [2001]	101
Baxter v Four Oaks Properties [1965]	114
Benn v Hardinge [1992]	107
Bernard v Josephs [1982]	51
Bernstein v Skyviews and General Ltd [1978]	3
Bettison v Langton [2002]	99
Biggs v Hoddinott [1898]	89

TABLE OF CASES

Billson v Residential Apartments Ltd [1992]	81
Binions v Evans [1972]	59
Bostock v Bryant [1990]	74
Bristol & West Building Society v Henning [1985]	27
British Railways Board v Glass [1965]	101
Bruton v London and Quadrant Housing Trust [1999]	78
Buchanan-Wollaston's Conveyance, Re [1939]	53, 126
Buckingham CC v Moran [1990]	34
Bull v Bull [1955]	47, 124
Burgess v Rawnsley [1975]	50
Burns v Burns [1984]	59
Burns v Morton [1999]	38
Calabar Properties Ltd v Stitcher [1984]	82
Campbell v Griffith [2001]	46
Carr-Glynn v Frearsons [1998]	48
Carr v Issard [2006]	46
CDC2020 v Ferreira [2005]	107
Central London Commercial States Ltd v Kato Kagaku Co Ltd [1998]	37
Cheltenham and Gloucester BS v Norgan [1996]	93
CIBC Mortgages plc v Pitt [1994]	91
Cityland and Property (Holdings) Ltd v Dabrah [1968]	89
City of London Corp v Fell [1993]	79
City of London Building Society v Flegg [1988]	27, 60
Claughton v Charalambous [1998]	54
Cobbe v Yeoman's Row Management [2008]	62
Colchester BC v Smith [1992]	34
Colls v Home and Colonial Stores Ltd [1904]	101
Co-operative Insurance Society Ltd v Argyll Stores Ltd [1998]	80
Copeland v Greenhalf [1952]	100
Crabb v Arun DC [1976]	61
Crago v Julien [1992]	70
Crest Nicholson Residential Ltd v McAllister [2004]	112
Crow v Wood [1971]	100
Cuckmere Brick Co Ltd v Mutual Finance [1971]	93

TABLE OF CASES

Curley v Parkes [2004]	56, 59, 64
Dalton v Angus and Co [1881]	105
Dano Ltd v Earl Cadogen [2003]	115
Das v Linden Mews Ltd [2002]	101
Dean v Allin & Watts [2001]	87
Dennis, Re [1995]	50
D'Eyncourt v Gregory [1886]	4
Diamond and Sandham [2004]	83
Diligent Finance Co v Alleyne [1972]	16
Dolphin's Conveyance, Re [1970]	114
Dowty Boulton Paul Ltd v Wolverhampton Corp (No 2) [1976]	98
Drake v Whipp [1995]	57
Dunbar Bank plc v Nadeem [1998]	91
Du Sautoy v Symes [1967]	15
Dyce v Lady James Hay [1852]	100
Eaton Square Properties Ltd v O'Higgins [2000]	78
Edginton v Clark [1964]	34
Ellenborough Park, Re [1956]	98, 99, 102
Eller v Grovecrest Investments Ltd [1995]	82
Elliston v Reacher [1908]	113
Equity & Law Home Loans Ltd v Prestidge [1992]	27
ER Ives Ltd v High [1967]	103
Errington v Errington and Woods [1952]	65
Eves v Eves [1975]	59
Facchini v Bryson [1952]	75
Fairclough v Swan Brewery Co Ltd [1912]	88
Fairweather v St Marylebone Property Trust Ltd [1963]	37
Family Housing Association v Jones [1990]	78
Federated Homes Ltd v Mill Lodge Properties Ltd [1980]	112
First National Bank plc v Achampong [2003]	53
First National Securities Ltd v Hegerty [1985]	50
Four-Maids Ltd v Dudley Marshall Ltd [1957]	93

TABLE OF CASES

Fowler v Barron [2008]	47, 59
Fuller v Happy Shopper Markets Ltd [2001]	81
Gerrard v Cooke [1806]	100
Gillett v Holt [2000]	61
Gissing v Gissing [1971]	59
Goodman v Gallant [1986]	51
Gotobed v Pridmore [1970]	107
Grant v Edwards [1986]	59, 64
Gray v Taylor [1998]	75, 78
Greasley v Cooke [1980]	61
Greenwich Health Care NHS Trust v London & Quadrant Housing Trust [1998]	106
Grigsby v Melville [1974]	100
Hair v Gillman [2000]	104
Halifax Building Society v Thomas [1996]	93
Halsall v Brizell [1957]	116, 117
Hammersmith & Fulham LBC v Monk [1992]	83
Hammond v Mitchell [1991]	59
Harris v Flower [1904]	101
Haywood v Brunswick Permanent Benefit Building Society [1881]	115
Hill v Tupper [1863]	99
Hilton v Plustitle [1988]	78
Holaw (470) v Stockton Estates Ltd [2000]	106
Holbeck Hall Hotel Ltd v Scarborough BC [2000]	98
Holland v Hodgson [1872]	3
Holliday, Re [1981]	54
Horrill v Cooper [1998]	15
Horsham Properties Group Ltd v Clark [2008]	94
Hunt v Luck [1902]	8
Hussey v Palmer [1972]	59
Ingram v IRC [1999]	74
In the Estate of Crippen [1911]	50
Ives v High [1967]	17, 61, 63

TABLE OF CASES

Jamaica Life Assurance Society v Hillsborough Ltd [1989]	114
James Jones Ltd v Earl of Tankerville [1909]	65
J A Pye (Oxford) Ltd v Graham [2001]	33
J A Pye (Oxford) Land Ltd v the United Kingdom [2007]	35
Javad v Aqil [1991]	70
Jelbert v Davis [1968]	101
Jennings v Rice [2002]	61
Jeune v Queens Cross Properties [1974]	82
Jones v Challenger [1961]	53
Jones v Stones [1999]	38
Joyce v Rigolli [2004]	38
K, Re [1986]	50
Kinch v Bullard [1999]	49
King v David Allen Ltd [1916]	65
Kingsnorth Finance Co Ltd v Tizard [1986]	8, 60
Kings North Trust Ltd v Bell [1986]	90
Knightsbridge Estates Trust Ltd v Byrne [1940]	88
Kreglinger v New Patagonia Meat and Cold Storage Co [1914]	89, 90
Lace v Chantler [1944]	74
Laiqat v Majid [2005]	3
Lake v Craddock [1955]	47, 124
Lambeth LBC v Blackburn [2001]	32
Lasker v Lasker [2008]	48
Leakey v National Trust [1980]	98
Le Foe v Le Foe [2001]	27, 58
Lloyds Bank plc v Rosset [1991]	56, 57
Lockwood v Wood [1844]	98
Loder v Gaden [1999]	101
London & Blenheim Estates Ltd v Ladbroke Retail Parks Ltd [1994]	101, 102
London CC v Allen [1914]	115
Lyus v Prowsa Developments Ltd [1982]	59
Malayan Credit Ltd v Jack Chia-MPH Ltd [1986]	47, 124

TABLE OF CASES

Mancetter Developments v Garmanson [1986]	4
Mannai Investment Co v Eagle Star Life Assurance Co Ltd [1997]	83
Marcroft Wagons Ltd v Smith [1951]	75
Marden v Heyes [1972]	79
McCall v Abelesz [1976]	79
Medforth v Blake [1999]	94
Mercer v Denne [1905]	98
Midland Bank v Cooke [1995]	58
Midland Bank v Farmpride Hatcheries [1981]	8
Midland Bank Trust Co v Green [1981]	15
Midtown Ltd v City of London Real Property Co Ltd [2005]	101
Mikeover v Brady [1989]	77
Miles v Easter [1933]	112
Miller v Emcer Products [1956]	98
Miller v Hancock [1893]	100
Mills v Silver [1991]	101
Mint v Good [1951]	79
Moncrieff v Jamieson [2007]	101
Moran [1990]	34
Mortgage Corp Ltd v Shaire [2001]	53
Mortgage Corp Ltd v Ubah [1997]	76
Moule v Garrett [1872]	79
Mouncey v Ismay [1865]	99
Mount Carmel Investments Ltd v Peter Thurlow Ltd [1988]	34
Multiservice Bookbinding Ltd v Marden [1979]	89
Mulvaney v Gough [2002]	99
National Car Parks Ltd v Trinity Development Co Ltd [2001]	74
National Carriers Ltd v Panalpina Ltd [1981]	83
Newham LBC v Hawkins [2005]	75
Nicholls v Lan [2006]	54
Nickerson v Barraclough [1981]	103
Nielson-Jones v Fedden [1975]	51
Noakes and Co Ltd v Rice [1902]	89
Norris v Checksfield [1991]	75

Case	Page
Notting Hill Housing Trust v Brackley [2001]	83
Oak Co-operative Building Society v Blackburn [1968]	16
Ofulue v Bossert [2008]	35
Oliver v Saunders Developments Ltd [2006]	114
Otter v Norman [1989]	75
Oxley v Hiscock [2004]	57, 58, 59, 64
Paddington Building Society v Mendelsohn [1985]	27
P & A Swift v Combined English Stores Group [1989]	79
P & S Platt v Crouch [2005]	105
Paragon Finance plc v Nash [2001]	89
Pascoe v Turner [1979]	61, 62
Peacock v Custins [2002]	101
Pearson v IRC [1981]	9
Peckham v Ellison [1998]	106
Pettitt v Pettitt [1970]	56
Petty v Styward [1631]	47
Powell v McFarlane [1977]	32, 34
Prudential Assurance Co v London Residuary Body [1992]	74
Pye v UK [2007]	35
R v Oxfordshire CC ex parte Sunningwell Parish Council [2000]	105
Rainbow Estates Ltd v Tokenhold [1999]	80
Red House Farm v Catchpole [1977]	34
Reeve v Lisle [1902]	88
Reid v Bickerstaff [1909]	113
Renals v Cowlishaw [1978]	112
Rhone v Stephens [1994]	116, 117
Ritchie v Ritchie [2007]	48
Roake v Chadha [1984]	112
Rodway v Landy [2001]	52
Roe v Siddons [1888]	99
Ropaigealach v Barclays Bank plc [1999]	93
Royal Bank of Scotland plc v Etridge (No 2) [2001]	91
Royal Bank of Scotland v Miller [2001]	93

TABLE OF CASES

Salih v Atchi [1961]	6
Samuel v Jarrah Timber and Wood Paving Corp Ltd [1904]	88
Santley v Wilde [1899]	86
Seton v Slade [1802]	87
Shah v Shah [2001]	10
Shaw's Application, Re [1995]	111
Shiloh Spinners v Harding [1973]	17
Simmonds v Dobson [1991]	105
Singla v Brown [2007]	51
Smith and Snipes Hall Farm v River Douglas Catchment Board [1949]	111, 112
Somma v Hazelhurst and Savelli [1978]	77
Sovmots Investments Ltd v S of S for the Environment [1979]	105
Spectrum Investment Co v Holmes [1981]	37
Spencer's Case [1583]	79
Springette v Defoe [1992]	56
Stack v Dowden [2007]	45, 58, 59
Standard Property Investments plc v British Plastics Federation [1987]	14
State Bank of India v Sood [1997]	61
Stewart v Scottish Widows & Life Assurance plc [2005]	79
Stirling v Leadenhall Residential 2 Ltd [2001]	75
Street v Mountford [1985]	73, 76, 77
Stribling v Wickham [1989]	77
Stuart v Joy [1904]	79
Supperstone v Hurst [2005]	45
Surrey CC v Bredero Homes Ltd [1993]	118
Surrey CC v Lamond [1998]	75
Sweet v Sommer [2004]	106
Swindon BC v Aston [2002]	75
Target Home Loans Ltd v Clothier [1994]	93
Taylor's Fashions Ltd v Liverpool Victoria Trustees Co Ltd [1982]	61
Thamesmead Town Ltd v Allotey [1998]	117

The Prior's Case [1368]	111
Thomas v Fuller-Brown [1988]	59
Tophams v Earl of Sefton [1967]	117
TSB Bank v Botham [1996]	3
TSB Bank v Camfield [1995]	92
Tulk v Moxhay [1848]	80, 115, 116
Union Lighterage Co v London Graving Dock Co [1902]	106
United Bank of Kuwait v Sahib [1997]	87
United Scientific Holdings v Burnley BC [1977]	79
Uratemp Ventures Ltd v Collins [2001]	78
Virdi v Chana [2008]	101
Walsh v Lonsdale [1882]	70, 87, 103
Webb's Lease, Re [1951]	106
Westminster CC v Clarke [1992]	78
Wheeldon v Burrows [1879]	99, 104, 105
Wheeler v JJ Saunders Ltd [1995]	104
White v Bijou Mansions [1938]	111
Williams & Glyn's Bank Ltd v Boland [1981]	26
Williams v Hensman [1861]	50
Williams v Jones [2002]	34
Williams v Kiley [2002]	114
Winter Garden Theatre Ltd v Millennium Productions Ltd [1948]	65
Wollerton and Wilson Ltd v Richard Costain Ltd [1970]	3
Wong v Beaumont Property Trust Ltd [1965]	103
Woolls v Powling [1999]	38
Wright v Macadam [1949]	104
Wrotham Park Estate Ltd v Parkside Homes Ltd [1974]	118
WX Investments v Begg [2002]	49
Yaxley v Gotts [2000]	10, 61, 71

Table of Statutes

Access to Neighbouring Land Act 1992	13, 103
Administration of Estates Act 1925—	
s 33	42
Administration of Justice Act 1970—	
s 36	93
Agricultural Holdings Act 1986	72
Agricultural Tenancies Act 1995	72
Commonhold and Leasehold Reform Act 2002	117
Common Law Procedure Act 1852	81
Consumer Credit Act 2006—	
ss 19–22	89
Contracts (Rights of Third Parties) Act 1999	111
Civil Aviation Act 1982	3
Deeds of Arrangement Act 1914	14
Family Law Act 1966	14
Financial Service and Markets Act 2000	89
Forfeiture Act 1982—	
s 2	50
Housing Act 1985	73
Housing Act 1988	73
Housing Act 1996	73
Inclosure Acts	103
Inheritance (Provision for Family and Dependants) Act 1975	50

TABLE OF STATUTES

Insolvency Act 1986–	
s 335A	54
Interpretation Act 1978–	
Sch 1	2
Land Charges Act 1925	13
Land Charges Act 1972	12–15
s 2(4)	14, 72
s 2(5)–(7)	14
s 4	15
s 4(6)	15
s 10(4)	15
Landlord and Tenant Act 1954–	
Pt II	72, 78
Landlord and Tenant Act 1985–	
s 1	79
s 8	79
s 11	78
s 17	82
Landlord and Tenant (Covenants) Act 1995	80
s 2(1)	80
s 3	80
s 3(6)	80
s 4	80
s 5	80
s 6	80
s 7	80
s 8	80
s 16	80
Land Registration Act 1925	26, 34
s 70(1)(f)	34
s 70(1)(g)	26
s 75	34
Land Registration Act 2002	20, 25, 123–25
Pt 8	21
s 3	22

s 4	22, 72
s 9	23
s 10	23
s 23(1)	86
s 25	121
s 27(1)	20
s 29	22
ss 32–36	23
ss 40–47	24
s 44	42, 123
s 60	37
s 65	124
s 71(a)	25
s 116	63
s 117	25
s 132(1)	2
Sch 1	22, 24
Sch 1, paras 1, 2	72
Sch 1, para 3	106
Sch 3	22, 24
Sch 3, para 1	72
Sch 3, para 2	25, 72
Sch 3, para 3	106
Sch 3, para 4	98
Sch 3, para 5	98
Sch 4	21, 28
Sch 5	21
Sch 6	35
Sch 6, para 1	36
Sch 6, para 2	36
Sch 6, para 3	36
Sch 6, para 5	36, 38
Sch 6, para 6	36
Sch 6, para 7	36
Sch 6, para 13	36
Sch 8	21, 29

TABLE OF STATUTES

Land Registration Rules 2003	20, 21, 23, 37
Pt 7	23
Law of Property Act 1925	12, 44
s 1	6
s 1(1)	6, 68
s 1(2)	6
s 1(3)	6
s 1(2)(a)	103
s 1(6)	42, 44, 46, 123, 124
s 2	21, 52, 60
s 27	21, 28, 52, 60
s 30	53
ss 34–36	42, 123
s 34(2)	44, 45, 123
s 36(2)	44, 48, 49, 123, 124
s 52(1)	10, 70
s 53(1)(b)	42, 56
s 53(1)(c)	87
s 53(2)	42, 56
s 54(2)	70
s 56	111
s 62	104
s 62(1)	3, 5
s 62(4)	3, 5, 102
s 77	79
s 78	111–113
s 79	116, 117
s 84(1)	118
s 85(1), (2)	86
s 86(1)	86
s 86(2)	87
s 87(1)	86, 87
s 88	94

s 89	94
s 91(2)	92
s 101	92
s 101(1)	94
s 103	93
s 109	94
s 141	80
s 142	80
s 146	81
s 153	83
s 153(1)	117
s 196	49
s 196(3)	49
s 196(4)	49, 50
s 198	8
s 198(1)	14
s 199	8
s 205(1)(ix)	2
s 205(1)(xix)	9
s 205(1)(xxvii)	68
Sch 1	61
Sch 3, para 2	61
Law of Property Act 1969	12
s 23	12, 15
Law of Property (Miscellaneous Provisions) Act 1989—	
s 1	10
s 2	9, 10, 12, 38, 70, 87
s 2(5)	10
Limitation Act 1980	34
s 15(1)	34
s 19	80
s 20(1)	92
s 20(5)	92
Sch 1	34
Local Land Charges Act 1975	16

TABLE OF STATUTES

Matrimonial Causes Act 1973–	
s 24	51
Party Wall etc Act 1996	38
s 1	38
ss 3–5	39
s 7	39
Prescription Act 1832	105
s 1	105
s 2	105
s 3	105
s 4	105
Protection from Eviction Act 1977–	
s 2	81
s 5	69
Rent Act 1977	72, 76–78
Rent Acts	73, 76, 77, 78
Rentcharges Act 1977–	
s 2(3)(c)	117
Settled Land Act 1925	43
s 18	13
s 72	13
Supreme Court Act 1981–	
s 37(1)	94
s 50	118
Trustee Act 1925–	
s 34(2)	44
Trusts of Land and Appointment of Trustees Act 1996	52
s 1	42, 44
s 2	43
s 4	2, 44
s 5	44
s 6(1)	45
s 7	45

s 8	45
s 10	45
s 11	45
s 12(1)	52
s 13	52
s 13(2)	52
s 13(4)	52
s 13(6)	52
s 14	52
s 15	52
s 15(1)(a)–(d)	53
s 15(3)	53
Sch 1	43
Sch 4	2
Treasure Act 1996	3

Table of Statutory Instruments

Land Registration Rules 2003, SI 2003/1417	20
Pt 2	21
Pt 7	23
Pt 10	21, 37
r 5	21
r 8	21
r 9	21
r 189	36
Registration of Title Order 1989, SI 1989/1347	12

Table of European Legislation

Conventions and Treaties

EEC 1957 (Treaty of Rome)—
  Art 81   89
European Convention for the Protection of Human Rights   81
  and Fundamental Freedoms 1950
  Protocol No.1, Art 1   35

Abbreviations

Titles of Acts and Rules used repeatedly in the text are abbreviated as follows. (Their dates are given in the text.)

AEA	Administration of Estates Act
AJA	Administration of Justice Act
CAA	Civil Aviation Act
CPR	Civil Procedure Rules
C(ROTP)A	Contacts (Rights Of Third Parties) Act
HA	Housing Act
LA	Limitation Act
LCA	Land Charges Act
LPA	Law of Property Act
LP(MP)A	Law of Property (Miscellaneous Provisions) Act
LRA	Land Registration Act
LRR	Land Registration Rules
LTA	Landlord and Tenant Act
LT(C)A	Landlord and Tenant (Covenants) Act
PEA	Protection from Eviction Act
RA	Rent Act
SLA	Settled Land Act
TA	Trustee Act
TCPA	Town and Country Planning Act
TOLATA	Trusts of Land and Appointment of Trustees Act
WA	Wills Act

How to use this book

Welcome to this new edition of Routledge Land Lawcards. In response to student feedback, we've added some new features to these new editions to give you all the support and preparation you need in order to face your law exams with confidence.

Inside this book you will find:

■ NEW tables of cases and statutes for ease of reference

Table of Cases

Aluminium Industrie Vaasen v Romalpa Aluminium Ltd [1976] 1 WLR 676	14, 15
Andrews v Hopkinson [1956] 3 All ER 422	138
Armour v Thyssen [1990] 3 All ER 481	13
Armstrong v Jackson [1917] 2 KB 822	115
Ashington Piggeries v Hill [1971] 1 All ER 847	53
Barber v NWS Bank [1996] 1 All ER 906	37
Barrow Lane and Ballard v Phillips [1929] 1 KB 574	18, 19
Bartlett v Sidney Marcus [1965] 2 All ER 753	56
Bence Graphics International Ltd v Fasson UK [1998] QB 87	103, 184
Bentinck v Cromwell Engineering [1971] 1 QB 324	172, 173
Bowmakers v Barnett Instruments [1945] KB 65	171, 172
Branwhite v Worcester Works Finance [1969] 1 AC 552	140
Bunge Corporation v Tradax [1981] 2 All ER 513	120
Butterworth v Kingsway Motors [1954] 1 WLR 1286	37
Car and Universal Finance v Caldwell [1965] 1 QB 31	27
Central Newbury Car Auctions v Unity Finance [1957] 1 QB 371	25
Charge Card Services Ltd, Re [1988] 3 All ER 702	92
Clegg v Ole Andersson [2003] 1 All ER 721	66
Clough Mill v Martin [1985] 1 WLR 111	16
Colley v Overseas Exporters [1921] 3 KB 302	121
Couturier v Hastie [1856] 5 HL Cas 673	18
Cundy v Lindsay [1878] 3 App Cas 459	27
Demby Hamilton Ltd v Barden [1949] 1 All ER 435	11
Dimond v Lovell [2000] 2 All ER 897	153
Director General of Fair Trading v First National Bank [2001] 1 All ER 97	83, 185

Table of Statutes

Companies Act 1985	
s 395	14
Companies Act 2006	
s 860	14
Consumer Credit Act 1956	112
Consumer Credit Act 1974	2, 30, 31, 84, 112, 128, 130, 144, 145, 147, 150, 151, 154, 156, 168
s 8	129, 153
s 9(1)	129
s 11	134
s 12	134
s 15	131
s 17	134
s 19	135
s 33	173
s 34	173
s 39	145
s 39A	145
s 40	145
s 46	147
s 48	145
s 49	147
s 49(1)	145
ss 50–1	147

xxix

HOW TO USE THIS BOOK

■ Revision Checklists

We've summarised the key topics you will need to know for your law exams and broken them down into a handy revision checklist. Check them out at the beginning of each chapter, then after you have the chapter down, revisit the checklist and tick each topic off as you gain knowledge and confidence.

1

Sources of law

Primary legislation: Acts of Parliament	☐
Secondary legislation	☐
Case law	☐
System of precedent	☐
Common law	☐
Equity	☐
EU law	☐
Human Rights Act 1998	☐

■ Key Cases

We've identified the key cases that are most likely to come up in exams. To help you to ensure that you can cite cases with ease, we've included a brief account of the case and judgment for a quick aide-memoire.

HENDY LENNOX v GRAHAME PUTTICK [1984]

Basic facts

Diesel engines were supplied, subject to a *Romalpa* clause, then fitted to generators. Each engine had a serial number. When the buyer became insolvent the seller sought to recover one engine. The Receiver argued that the process of fitting the engine to the generator passed property to the buyer. The court disagreed and allowed the seller to recover the still identifiable engine despite the fact that some hours of work would be required to disconnect it.

Relevance

If the property remains identifiable and is not irredeemably changed by the manufacturing process a *Romalpa* clause may be viable.

■ Companion Website

At the end of each chapter you will be prompted to visit the Routledge Lawcards companion website where you can test your understanding online with specially prepared multiple-choice questions, as well as revise the key terms with our online glossary.

You should now be confident that you would be able to tick all of the boxes on the checklist at the beginning of this chapter. To check your knowledge of Sources of law why not visit the companion website and take the Multiple Choice Question test. Check your understanding of the terms and vocabulary used in this chapter with the flashcard glossary.

HOW TO USE THIS BOOK

Exam Practice

Once you've acquired the basic knowledge, you'll want to put it to the test. The Routledge Questions and Answers provides examples of the kinds of questions that you will face in your exams, together with suggested answer plans and a fully-worked model answer. We've included one example free at the end of this book to help you put your technique and understanding into practice.

QUESTION 1

What are the main sources of law today?

Answer plan
This is, apparently, a very straightforward question, but the temptation is to ignore the European Community (EU) as a source of law and to over-emphasise custom as a source. The following structure does not make these mistakes:

- in the contemporary situation, it would not be improper to start with the EU as a source of UK law;

- then attention should be moved on to domestic sources of law: statute and common law;

- the increased use of delegated legislation should be emphasised;

- custom should be referred to, but its extremely limited operation must be emphasised.

ANSWER

European law
Since the UK joined the European Economic Community (EEC), now the EU, it has progressively but effectively passed the power to create laws which are operative in this country to the wider European institutions. The UK is now subject to Community law, not just as a direct consequence of the various treaties of accession passed by the UK Parliament, but increasingly, it is subject to the secondary legislation generated by the various institutions of the EU.

Fundamental concepts

Definitions of Land

Concept of Property

Test for fixture or chattel

Concept of tenure and estates

Concept of rights, estates and interests

Concept of notice

Concept of fee simple absolute in possession

Requirements for a valid contract for sale

Requirements for a valid conveyance of land

STATUTORY DEFINITIONS OF LAND

'Land' includes land of any tenure and mines and minerals, whether or not held apart from the surface, buildings or parts of buildings ... and other corporeal hereditaments; also a manor, an advowson, and a rent and other corporeal hereditaments, and an easement, right, privilege, or benefit in, over, or derived from land ... : (s 205(1)(ix) of the LPA 1925, amended by Sched 4 to the TOLATA 1996).

'Land includes buildings and other structures, land covered with water, and any estate, interest, easement, servitude or right in or over land: (Sched 1 to the Interpretation Act 1978).

■ Land includes–

(a) buildings and other structures
(b) land covered with water, and
(c) mines and minerals, whether or not held with the surface

(Section 132(1) of the LRA 2002).

■ 'Hereditament' refers to real property capable of being inherited.

Traditionally, ownership of land has been held to be ownership of a space from the highest heavens down to the centre of the earth, but this view has been

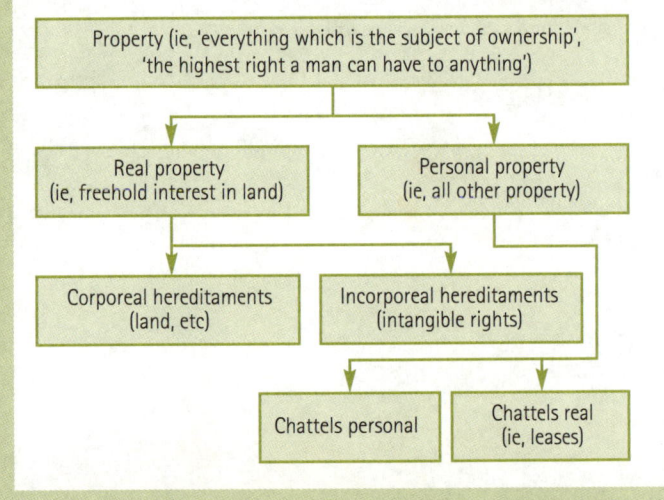

```
                Property (ie, 'everything which is the subject of ownership',
                        'the highest right a man can have to anything')
                                        │
                        ┌───────────────┴───────────────┐
                        ▼                               ▼
                  Real property                   Personal property
              (ie, freehold interest in land)     (ie, all other property)
                        │                               │
                        ▼                               ▼
              Corporeal hereditaments          Incorporeal hereditaments
                  (land, etc)                       (intangible rights)
                                                        │
                                        ┌───────────────┴───────────────┐
                                        ▼                               ▼
                                Chattels personal                 Chattels real
                                                                  (ie, leases)
```

modified by the requirements of modern life (see, for example, the CAA 1982; Treasure Act 1996; *Wollerton and Wilson Ltd v Richard Costain Ltd* [1970] – liability for overhanging crane jib; *Bernstein v Skyviews and General Ltd* [1978] – no liability in trespass for aircraft flying over land at a reasonable height; *Laiqat v Majid* [2005] – liability for extraction duct that encroached onto neighbouring land by 750 mm).

PROBLEMS OF PROPERTY ARISING WHERE CHATTELS ARE AFFIXED TO LAND

Problems may emerge from interpretation of the old maxim: 'Whatever is annexed to the soil becomes a part thereof.' Section 62(1) of the LPA 1925 tells us that all fixtures are conveyed with the land, unless there is a contrary intention expressed in the conveyance (s 62(4)). How do we decide whether or not an item is a fixture? (See figure on p. 4.)

▶ HOLLAND v HODGSON [1872]

The test for a fixture or chattel will depend upon the degree and purpose of annexation. The question is whether the chattel has been fixed to the land for better enjoyment of the chattel, or to enhance the use of the land.

Facts

Upon repossession of a factory, the mortgagee claimed ownership of some spinning looms which were bolted to the floor.

Held

The looms were fixtures and formed part of the land. Articles resting on their own weight are not regarded as part of the land unless a contrary intention can be shown and articles attached to the land are to be regarded as part of the land unless it can be shown that they were intended to constitute a chattel.

Fixtures may be removed lawfully from land in the cases of:

- *Mortgagor and mortgagee* – where land has been mortgaged, fixtures may be included in the mortgage. (*TSB Bank v Botham* [1996]).

FUNDAMENTAL CONCEPTS

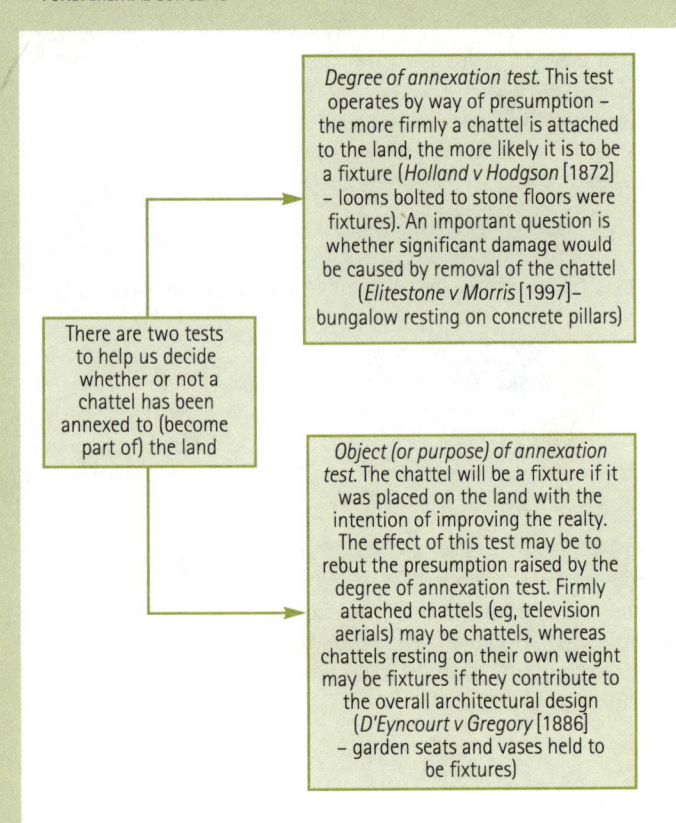

There are two tests to help us decide whether or not a chattel has been annexed to (become part of) the land

→ *Degree of annexation test.* This test operates by way of presumption – the more firmly a chattel is attached to the land, the more likely it is to be a fixture (*Holland v Hodgson* [1872] – looms bolted to stone floors were fixtures). An important question is whether significant damage would be caused by removal of the chattel (*Elitestone v Morris* [1997] – bungalow resting on concrete pillars)

→ *Object (or purpose) of annexation test.* The chattel will be a fixture if it was placed on the land with the intention of improving the realty. The effect of this test may be to rebut the presumption raised by the degree of annexation test. Firmly attached chattels (eg, television aerials) may be chattels, whereas chattels resting on their own weight may be fixtures if they contribute to the overall architectural design (*D'Eyncourt v Gregory* [1886] – garden seats and vases held to be fixtures)

■ *Landlord and tenant* – in general, the landlord is entitled to fixtures attached by the tenant. There are exceptions in cases of agricultural fixtures, trade fixtures (which may be removed before but not after the end of tenancy), and ornamental fixtures (which can be removed without causing substantial injury to property).

There is a common law duty to make good any damage caused by removal of tenants' fixtures and to leave the premises in reasonable condition. Liability at common law is on the person who removed the fixtures (*Mancetter Developments v Garmanson* [1986]).

■ *Vendor and purchaser* – under a conveyance, fixtures pass to a purchaser without express mention (s 62(1) of the LPA 1925), unless there is a contrary intention expressed in the conveyance (s 62(4)).

> ### D'EYNCOURT v GREGORY [1886]
>
> **Where an object is annexed to enhance the land rather than for its enjoyment, the object will constitute a fixture.**
>
> Facts
>
> A dispute arose over a number of items that the purchaser claimed were fixtures and should remain with the property. The items included:
>
> - Stone statues resting on their own weight
> - Tapestries fixed to the walls, and
> - Vases
>
> Held
>
> The items were fixtures on the basis that they constituted part of the architectural design of the house. The annexation was to enhance the land itself rather than to enjoy the chattel as an individual object.

CONCEPT OF TENURE AND ESTATES

Tenure is concerned with the conditions upon which land is held. It answers the question: *how* is land held? Today, all land is held by the Crown, directly or indirectly. *Estate* is concerned with the length of time for which a tenant may hold land. It answers the question: for *how long* is land held?

CONCEPTS OF RIGHTS, ESTATES AND INTERESTS

Generally speaking, when you hold an estate in the land you have 'ownership' of the land. If you have an interest in land you have an interest (for example, a right of way) in or over land owned by somebody else.

Legal rights are rights *in rem*, binding 'the entire world'. *Equitable rights* can be proprietary or in personam. They bind all persons other than the *bona fide* purchaser of a legal estate without notice of such (equitable) rights.

FUNDAMENTAL CONCEPTS

Section 1 of the LPA 1925

Section 1(1)
Only two legal estates: fee simple absolute in possession – freehold – lasts virtually for ever; term of years absolute – leasehold – lasts for some determinate period (a week, a month, a thousand years, etc)

Section 1(2)
Only five interests which may be legal (ie, these interests may be legal or equitable): easement; rentcharge; charge by way of legal mortgage; any other similar charge created by instrument; rights of entry exercisable over a legal lease or rentcharge

Section 1(3)
'All other estates, interests and charges in or over land take effect as equitable interests'

CONCEPT OF 'PURCHASER WITHOUT NOTICE'

An equitable interest may be enforced against all persons, *except* a *bona fide* purchaser, for value of the legal estate, who has taken without notice of the existence of that interest, and against one who claims through him:

- '*Bona fide*' – the purchaser must have acted in good faith and without fraud.

- '*Purchaser*' – one who takes property by sale or gift, and not merely by operation of law (as on an intestacy). Includes mortgagee and lessee.

- '*Value*' – refers to any consideration in money, money's worth, or consideration of a future marriage (*Salih v Atchi* [1961]). Should the purchaser acquire a legal estate and not give value, he will take subject to all existing equitable rights.

- '*Legal estate*' – this refers to legal fee simple absolute or legal term of years.

CONCEPT OF TENURE AND ESTATES

- '*Without notice*' – a purchaser with notice of the equitable interest will usually take the estate subject to that interest.

> ### ▶ HUNT v LUCK [1902]
>
> **A purchaser will be fixed with constructive notice of any equitable interest owned by a person in possession unless enquiry is made of that person and he does not reveal his interest.**
>
> Facts
>
> Mrs H believed that certain conveyances purportedly made by her late husband were forgeries. The people to whom the properties had been mortgaged argued that they were *bona fide* purchasers without notice. Mrs H claimed that the mortgagees were under a duty to make such enquiries as a prudent, careful and reasonable man would have made.
>
> Held
>
> The mortgagees were held to be purchasers for value without notice whose title had to prevail over that of the plaintiff. A purchaser will be regarded as having knowledge of anything a prudent purchaser would have discovered by inspecting the land and the title deeds.

'Notice' refers to awareness of some event or state of affairs. It does not include giving one's attention to vague rumours (*Barnhart v Greenshields* [1853]). The doctrine of notice applies only to land with unregistered title. 'The law as to notice … has no application even by analogy to registered land' (*Williams & Glyns Bank v Boland* [1981], per Lord Wilberforce).

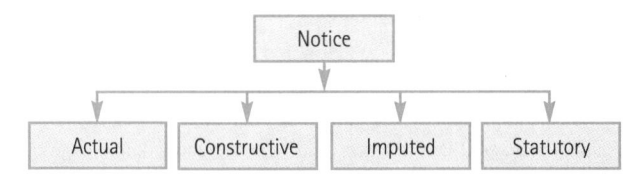

```
                    Notice
        ┌──────┬──────┴──────┬──────────┐
      Actual  Constructive  Imputed   Statutory
```

Actual notice – the purchaser is made expressly aware during negotiations of some prior equitable interest. Since 1926, actual notice has only applied to residual interests in unregistered land. A residual equitable interest is one that is neither overreachable nor capable of entry in the Land Charges Register.

Constructive notice – the purchaser is deemed to have been given such notice if he could have discovered the interest had he made the appropriate inquiries, for example, by inspecting the land (see *Hunt v Luck* [1902]) – purchaser fixed with constructive notice of the rights of those in occupation of the land); s 199 of the LPA 1925. Such notice may be presumed where there has been express notice of a fact which ought to have led to notice of other facts (see *Midland Bank v Farmpride Hatcheries* [1981]). Constructive notice applies only to residual interests in unregistered land.

Imputed notice – the purchaser employs a solicitor or other agent, and their notice of claims is imputed to the purchaser (*Kingsnorth Finance Co Ltd v Tizard* [1986]). Imputed notice also only applies to residual interests in unregistered land.

Statutory notice – statutory notice applies only to those interests in unregistered land which are capable of entry in the Land Charges Register. Section 198 of the LPA 1925 provides that registration of an interest in the Land Charges Register constitutes actual notice to all persons and for all purposes.

▶ KINGSNORTH FINANCE CO v TIZARD [1986]

A purchaser will be fixed with constructive notice of any rights which would have been discoverable if reasonable enquiries had been made.

Facts

The mortgagor stated in his application that he was single. He told an agent of the bank that he was separated from his spouse. There was evidence that children were in occupation, but the agent made no further enquiries.

Held

The bank was bound by the equitable interest of the mortgagor's spouse. Their agent was deemed to have constructive knowledge of the interest, and that knowledge was imputed on the bank.

CONCEPT OF THE FEE SIMPLE ABSOLUTE IN POSSESSION

The largest estate known to English land law involves unlimited duration in time, with extensive powers over the land. It is known also as 'freehold estate':

- '*Fee*' denotes estate of inheritance, that is, it will not necessarily end on death of the owner. It will end only on failure of an appropriate successor in title.

- '*Simple*' denotes an ordinary fee capable of passing to general heirs and which carries no condition as to passing to one particular class of heir.

- '*Absolute*' denotes that the estate is not limited in time. A fee simple may not be absolute, for example, it is possible to create a determinable fee (one that will never determine unless something happens – eg, a fee simple until the United Kingdom leaves the European Union), or a conditional fee (one that will last for as long as a condition is complied with – eg, a fee to X and his heirs for as long as they reside in the property).

- '*In possession*' denotes an estate which is immediate, and, therefore, neither in reversion nor remainder. The phrase bestows 'a present right of present enjoyment' (see *Pearson v IRC* [1981]). It includes receipt of rents, profits, and the right to receive same: s 205(1)(xix) of the LPA 1925. ('Reversion': rights retained by grantor; 'remainder' – present right to some future enjoyment of land.)

CREATION AND TRANSFER OF ESTATES AND INTERESTS IN LAND

Requirements for a valid contract for sale

Section 2 of the LP(MP)A 1989
Contracts after 26 September 1989
Contract writing
Containing all terms expressly agreed
Signed by all parties

(*Continued*)

Section 2 of the LP(MP)A 1989
Exceptions: resulting, implied or constructive trusts (s 2(5)); estoppel? – see *Yaxley v Gotts* [2000] and *Banner v Luff Developments* [2000]
Otherwise, contract void

Requirements for a valid conveyance of land

All conveyances must be by deed (see s 52(1) of the LPA 1925).

After 30 July 1990, deeds must be:
● signed; ● delivered; ● witnessed; ● see s 1 of the LP(MP)A 1989; ● *Exception*: estoppel (see *Shah v Shah* [2001]).

You should now be confident that you would be able to tick all the boxes on the checklist at the beginning of this chapter. To check your knowledge of Fundamental concepts why not visit the companion website and take the Multiple Choice Question test. Check your understanding of the terms and vocabulary used in this chapter with the flashcard glossary.

2

Conveying title to land with unregistered title

Legal and equitable interests in unregistered land	☐
Overreaching beneficial interests in unregistered land	☐
Registration of Land Charges	☐
Land Charges Register	☐
Residual interests	☐

CONVEYING TITLE TO LAND WITH UNREGISTERED TITLE

Almost 20 per cent of the land in England and Wales remains unregistered. The law concerning unregistered conveyancing is to be found in the common law, as modified by such statutes as the LPA 1925, the LPA 1969 and the LCA 1972.

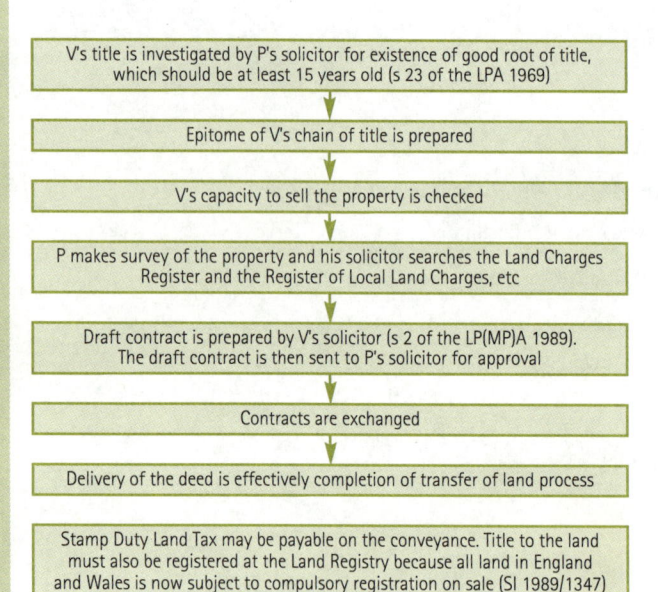

(V = vendor; P = purchaser)

```
┌─────────────────────────────────────────────────────────────────┐
│ V's title is investigated by P's solicitor for existence of good│
│ root of title, which should be at least 15 years old (s 23 of   │
│ the LPA 1969)                                                   │
└─────────────────────────────────────────────────────────────────┘
                              ▼
┌─────────────────────────────────────────────────────────────────┐
│ Epitome of V's chain of title is prepared                       │
└─────────────────────────────────────────────────────────────────┘
                              ▼
┌─────────────────────────────────────────────────────────────────┐
│ V's capacity to sell the property is checked                    │
└─────────────────────────────────────────────────────────────────┘
                              ▼
┌─────────────────────────────────────────────────────────────────┐
│ P makes survey of the property and his solicitor searches the   │
│ Land Charges Register and the Register of Local Land Charges,etc│
└─────────────────────────────────────────────────────────────────┘
                              ▼
┌─────────────────────────────────────────────────────────────────┐
│ Draft contract is prepared by V's solicitor (s 2 of the LP(MP)A │
│ 1989). The draft contract is then sent to P's solicitor for     │
│ approval                                                        │
└─────────────────────────────────────────────────────────────────┘
                              ▼
┌─────────────────────────────────────────────────────────────────┐
│ Contracts are exchanged                                         │
└─────────────────────────────────────────────────────────────────┘
                              ▼
┌─────────────────────────────────────────────────────────────────┐
│ Delivery of the deed is effectively completion of transfer of   │
│ land process                                                    │
└─────────────────────────────────────────────────────────────────┘

┌─────────────────────────────────────────────────────────────────┐
│ Stamp Duty Land Tax may be payable on the conveyance. Title to  │
│ the land must also be registered at the Land Registry because   │
│ all land in England and Wales is now subject to compulsory      │
│ registration on sale (SI 1989/1347)                             │
└─────────────────────────────────────────────────────────────────┘
```

WILL A PURCHASER BE BOUND BY INTERESTS IN UNREGISTERED LAND?

Legal rights, being rights *in rem*, will bind a purchaser.

Equitable rights are of three types (see figure opposite).

OVERREACHING BENEFICIAL INTERESTS IN UNREGISTERED LAND

Beneficial interests under a trust of land or strict settlement will be swept off the land and into the purchase money provided that:

■ In the case of a trust of land, a receipt for capital money is obtained from the trustees of land, being at least two in number or a trust corporation. A sole personal representative may also give a valid receipt.

Family equitable interests (ie, beneficial interests under a trust of land or strict settlement)	Subject to *overreaching* See ss 2 and 27 of the LPA1925; ss 18 and 72 of the SLA 1925
Commercial equitable interests	Protected by entry in the *Land Charges Register*
Residual equitable interests	Subject to the *doctrine of notice*

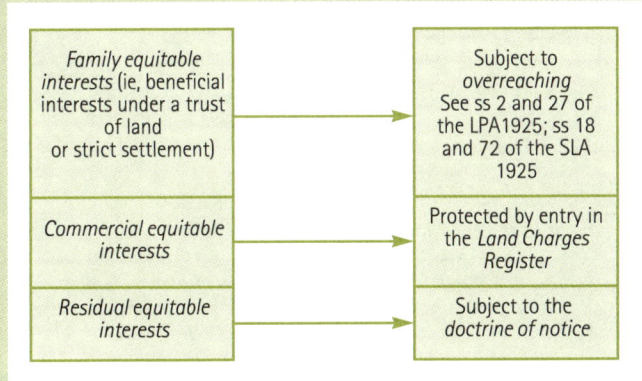

■ In the case of a strict settlement, the capital money is paid to the trustees, being at least two in number, or a trust corporation, or into court.

REGISTRATION OF LAND CHARGES

The system of registering land charges was introduced by the LCA 1925 (now LCA 1972). The system enables those who hold certain categories of interest in unregistered land to register the incumbrance in order to protect it against future purchasers of the land. The doctrine of notice no longer applies to these interests.

REGISTERS UNDER THE LCA 1972 (kept by Registrar at Land Charges Department of Land Registry)

Register of pending actions
Includes actions or proceedings pending in court, relating to land or any interest in or charge on land, and petitions in bankruptcy.

Register of Annuities
No further entries are to be made in this register.

Register of Writs and Orders Affecting Land
Includes writs or orders affecting land issued to enforce a judgment or recognisance, bankruptcy orders, access orders under Access to Neighbouring Land Act 1992.

Register of Deeds of Arrangement
Involves documents under which the debtor makes arrangements in favour of creditors: see Deeds of Arrangement Act 1914; s 7(1) of the LCA 1972.

Register of Land Charges
See below.

The six categories of Land Charges

Class A	LCA 1972, s 2(2)	Rents or annuities not created by deed
Class B	LCA 1972, s 2(3)	Land charges arising automatically by statute
Class C	LCA 1972, s 2(4)	C(i) puisne mortgages: legal mortgages not protected by deposit of title deeds C(ii) limited owner's charges C(iii) general equitable charges C(iv) estate contracts: includes options to purchase and rights of pre-emption
Class D	LCA 1972, s 2(5)	D(i) Inland Revenue charges D(ii) restrictive covenants created after 1925 D(iii) equitable easements created after 1925
Class E	LCA 1972, s 2(6)	Annuities created before 1926 and not registered in the Register of Annuities
Class F	LCA 1972, s 2(7)	Matrimonial home rights under the Family Law Act 1966. This provision enables a spouse who is not the legal owner of the land to register a right of occupation against the name of the legal owner

FEATURES OF THE LAND CHARGES REGISTER

- Registration is made against the name of the estate owner. The correct name of the estate owner is deemed to be the name used in the conveyancing documents (*Standard Property Investments plc v British Plastics Federation* [1987]).

- Registration constitutes actual notice to all persons and for all purposes (s 198(1) of the LPA 1925).

REGISTRATION OF LAND CHARGES

- An official search certificate is conclusive (s 10(4) of the LCA 1972).
- Unregistered interests which fall into Classes A, B, C(i)–(iii), E, and F are void as against a purchaser of the land charged with it (s 4 of the LCA 1972).

Unregistered interests which fall into Classes C(iv) and D will be void against a purchaser for money or money's worth (s 4(6) of the LCA 1972).

A purchaser of the legal estate will take free from an unregistered interest even if he has actual knowledge of it. Notice and good faith are irrelevant. In the words of Lord Wilberforce, 'it is not "fraud" to rely on legal rights conferred by Act of Parliament' (*Midland Bank Trust Co v Green* [1981]).

▶ MIDLAND BANK TRUST CO LTD v GREEN [1981]

An unregistered commercial equitable interest is void as against a purchaser irrespective of whether the purchaser has actual knowledge of the interest.

Facts

In 1961 a father granted to his son a ten-year option to purchase a farm for £22,500. The option was not registered as a class C(iv) land charge. In order to deprive his son of the option the father sold the farm to his wife for £500, which was significantly below its market value. The son then registered the option and attempted to enforce it.

Held

The option was void as against the mother due to non-registration, even though she knew about it.

Problems with the Land Charges Register

Interests which are registered against the name of somebody who owned the land prior to the first conveyance older than 15 years. Such interests are binding even though they may be undiscoverable when the purchaser investigates the vendor's title (see s 23 of the LPA 1969).

- Misdescription of the land either by the person entering the interest or by the vendor when searching the register (see *Du Sautoy v Symes* [1967] and *Horrill v Cooper* [1998]).

15

- Registration or searching under the wrong name (see *Oak Co-operative Building Society v Blackburn* [1968] and *Diligent Finance Co v Alleyne* [1972]).

> ### ▶ OAK CO-OPERATIVE BUILDING SOCIETY v BLACKBURN [1968]
>
> **In unregistered land a charge must be registered and the purchaser must search under the correct name.**
>
> Facts
>
> An option to purchase a property was registered as a class C(iv) land charge under the name of Frank David Blackburn – his business name. The plaintiff building society searched the Land Charges Register under the name Francis Davis Blackburn and obtained a certificate showing no entries under the name searched.
>
> Held
>
> The charge was effective against either a purchaser who did not search the register, or, as in this case, a purchaser who searched under the wrong name.

REGISTER OF LOCAL LAND CHARGES

This has nothing to do with the Land Charges Register.

- Applies to both registered and unregistered land.

- Each district council or London borough keeps its own register of local land charges under the Local Land Charges Act 1975.

- The registers include such matters as planning applications and restrictions, and charges for the making up of a road, etc.

- Entries are registered against the address of the property and not against the landowner.

RESIDUAL INTERESTS

These interests remain subject to the doctrine of notice.

- Easements and restrictive covenants created before 1926.

- Equitable mortgages protected by deposit of title deeds.

- Beneficial interests under a trust when there is only one trustee (see *Kingsnorth Finance Co v Tizard* [1986]).

- Estoppel licences (see *Ives v High* [1967]).

- Rights acquired by the doctrine of mutual benefit and burden (see *Halsall v Brizell* [1957]).

- Equitable rights of entry (see *Shiloh Spinners v Harding* [1973]).

You should now be confident that you would be able to tick all the boxes on the checklist at the beginning of this chapter. To check your knowledge of Conveying title to land with unregistered title why not visit the companion website and take the Multiple Choice Question test. Check your understanding of the terms and vocabulary used in this chapter with the flashcard glossary.

3

Transferring title to land with registered title

- Conveyancing process
- Principles underlying registered land
- Property, Proprietorship and Charges register
- Interests in registered land
- Registrable interests
- Classes of title
- Minor interests: methods of protection
- Overriding interests
- Alteration and indemnity of the register

TRANSFERRING TITLE TO LAND WITH REGISTERED TITLE

The law concerning land with registered title is to be found in the LRA 2002 and Land Registration Rules (LRR) 2003 (SI 2003/1417).

The conveyancing process is similar, but the following differences exist:

- Proof of title to the land is provided by registration at the Land Registry – not by deeds.

- The Land Charges Register and the doctrine of notice are irrelevant to registered land.

- An interest capable of substantive registration is identified by a unique title number and incumbrances are registered against the title – not against the name of the legal proprietor.

- The vendor's solicitor no longer has to prepare an abstract or epitome of title – title is verified by official copies of register entries.

A conveyance is now more correctly called a transfer.

See below for a comparison and summary of the different stages in unregistered and registered conveyancing.

Unregistered land	Registered land
Sale subject to contract (not legally binding)	Sale subject to contract (not legally binding)
Exchange of Contract	Exchange of Contract
Conveyance (legal title transferred)	Completion (land held on trust by vendor for purchaser)
Triggers compulsory registration (s 4(1) LRA 2002)	Registration of new proprietor (legal title transferred)

PRINCIPLES UNDERLYING REGISTERED LAND

Legal title does not pass from vendor to purchaser with conveyance or transfer – the purchaser only becomes the legal proprietor when the disposition is registered at the Land Registry (s 27(1) of the LRA 2002).

PRINCIPLES UNDERLYING REGISTERED LAND

Registered conveyancing is likely to change considerably when the proposals for electronic conveyancing are fully implemented. See Pt 8 and Sched 5 to the LRA 2002.

Mirror principle
The rights and interests shown on the register should mirror those existing on the land.

Curtain principle
The details of trusts are kept off the register (s 27 of the LPA 1925) – beneficial interests are overreached on sale (s 2 of the LPA 1925).

Insurance principle
The accuracy of the register is guaranteed by the State, and an indemnity may be available to injured parties (see Scheds 4 and 8 to the LRA 2002).

PARTS OF THE REGISTER

Property Register
Containing a description of the land and any benefits attached to that land; see r 5 of the LRR 2003.

The Property Register also contains a Title Plan, which is based upon the Ordnance Survey map. The purpose of the plan is to identify the land – it rarely provides evidence of the boundaries of the estate because the register shows general boundaries only (s 60 of the LRA 2002). Application may be made by the registered proprietor to have the exact line of the boundary fixed by the Registrar (see Pt 10 of the LRR 2003).

Proprietorship Register
Containing the name of the proprietor, the class of his title and any restrictions on his title: see r 8 of the LRR 2003.

Charges Register
Containing details of any changes or incumbrances on the land: see r 9 of the LRR 2003.

In addition to the above registers, the Land Registry is required to keep the following (see Pt 2 of the LRR 2003):

- an index map, which identifies and provides the title number for each plot of registered land;
- an index of proprietors' names.

INTERESTS IN REGISTERED LAND

Registrable interests
Obtain their own entry on the register – their own title number, etc.

Interests subject to an entry in the register
Commonly known as minor interests. Entered against the relevant title – anything apart from registrable interests may fall under this category. An interest will usually only bind a purchaser if it is recorded on the register [s 29 LRA 2002].

Interests which override a first disposition, and interests which override registered dispositions
Commonly known as overriding interests. These rights which will bind a purchaser whether they are on the register or not – for a list of overriding interests see Scheds 1 and 3 to the LRA 2002.

REGISTRABLE INTERESTS

Interests which must be registered
- Transfer of a freehold estate.
- Creation of a leasehold estate with more than seven years left to run.
- Granting of a legal charge over a freehold or leasehold for more than seven years.
- Expressly created legal easements.

See ss 4 and 27 of the LRA 2002.

Interests which may be registered
- Rentcharges;
- franchises;
- profits *à prendre* in gross. See s 3 of the LRA 2002.

CLASSES OF TITLE

Freehold title

- Absolute title: no apparent restrictions upon applicant's title.

- Qualified title: title established for a limited period or subject to reservations.

- Possessory title: applicant in actual possession of the land. See s 9 of the LRA 2002.

Leasehold title

- Absolute title: no apparent restrictions upon applicant's title, or the title of the lessor.

- Good leasehold title: no apparent restrictions on the applicant's title.

- Qualified title: title established for a limited period or subject to reservations.

- Possessory title: applicant in actual possession of the land. See s 10 of the LRA 2002.

MINOR INTERESTS: METHODS OF PROTECTION

Notices

Agreed notices: entered with the consent of the registered proprietor:

- The entry of a notice does not mean that the interest is valid.

- May not be entered in respect of a trust of land, a leasehold estate of less than three years, or a leasehold covenant.

See ss 32–34 of the LRA 2002.

Unilateral notices: entered without the consent of the registered proprietor: proprietor may apply for cancellation of the notice. See ss 35–36 of the LRA 2002 and Pt 7 of the Land Registration Rules (LRR).

Restrictions

Dealings with the land must be made in accordance with any restrictions. A restriction may be entered, for example, when there are two registered

TRANSFERRING TITLE TO LAND WITH REGISTERED TITLE

proprietors in order to ensure that the overreaching provisions are complied with. See ss 40–47 of the LRA 2002.

Overriding interests

Schedule 1 to the LRA 2002 (*Rights which override first registration*)	Schedule 3 to the LRA 2002 (*Rights which override registered dispositions*)
1 Leases not exceeding seven years	1 Leases not exceeding seven years
2 An interest belonging to a person in actual occupation of the land	2 An interest belonging to a person in actual occupation of the land (see below)
3 Legal easements and profits *à prendre*	3 Legal easements and profits *à prendre* (only if the right has been used within one year of the transfer, or it is within the actual knowledge of the transferee, or it would have been discoverable on a reasonably careful inspection of the land)
4 Customary rights	4 Customary rights
5 Public rights	5 Public rights
6 Local land charges	6 Local land charges
7 Rights to coal	7 Rights to coal
8 Rights to mines and minerals created before 1898	8 Rights to mines and minerals created before 1898
9 Rights to mines and minerals created 1898–1925	9 Rights to mines and minerals created 1898–1925
10 Franchises*	10 Franchises*
11 Manorial rights*	11 Manorial rights*
12 Rights to Crown rents*	12 Rights to Crown rents*
13 Rights in respect of embankments or sea walls*	13 Rights in respect of embankments or sea walls*

(*Continued*)

PRINCIPLES UNDERLYING REGISTERED LAND

14 Rights to payments in lieu of tithes*	14 Rights to payments in lieu of tithes*
15 Rights acquired by adverse possessions before 13/10/03	15 Rights acquired by adverse possessions before 13/10/03
16 Liability to repair the chancel of a church	16 Liability to repair the chancel of a church

* s 117 of the LRA 2002 provides that these rights will cease to have overriding status in 2013

Section 71(a) provides that anybody applying to register land must inform the registrar about any overriding interests of which he has knowledge. The effect of such disclosure will be that many overriding interests will be entered on the register, thereby losing their overriding status.

Paragraph 2 of Sched 3 (the rights of persons in actual occupation)

> **Does the person claiming the overriding interest have an interest in the land?**
> The right claimed must be an interest in the land (ie, not a licence). There can be no overriding interest if there is no interest in the first place! See *Lloyds Bank plc v Rosset* [1991]. Typical interests claimed by a person in actual occupation include: beneficial interests which have been acquired informally by way of resulting or constructive trust; options to purchase the land of which he is in actual occupation; and rights to renew a lease of the land of which he is in actual occupation

> **Is the person claiming the overriding interest in actual occupation of the land at the time of the disposition?**
> 'Actual' and 'occupation'are 'ordinary words of plain English and ... should be interpreted as such' (Lord Wilberforce in *Williams & Glyn's Bank v Boland* [1981]).
> The person claiming the interest must be in occupation of all of the land over which he claims an overriding interest because para 2 applies only 'so far as relating to land of which he is in occupation'

> **Did the purchaser have knowledge of that actual occupation or would it have been obvious on a reasonably careful inspection of the land?**
> This requirement has been added by the LRA 2002. It was not present under s 70(1)(g) of the LRA 1925 when the approach was 'if there is actual occupation and the occupier has rights, the purchaser takes subject to them. If not, he does not. No further element is material' (Lord Wilberforce in *Williams & Glyn's Bank v Boland* [1981])

> **Did the purchaser make inquiries of the person in actual occupation?**
> If the purchaser made inquiries of the person in actual occupation and the person in occupation failed to declare the fact that he has an interest in the land when he could reasonably have been expected to do so, the interest of the person in actual occupation will not bind the purchaser. For this reason, mortgagees make inquiries of, and often obtain waivers from, all people in occupation of the land to be mortgaged

Many of the problems concerning people in actual occupation of land have occurred when persons in occupation have nonoverreachable (one trustee) interests under resulting or constructive trusts and those interests have been held to bind a mortgagee, which has made no inquiry of the person in actual occupation. The interest in the land must have been acquired before the mortgage is granted to bind the mortgagee (*Williams & Glyn's Bank v Boland* [1981]).

▶ WILLIAMS AND GLYN'S BANK LTD v BOLAND [1981]

A beneficial interest under a trust is an interest in the land for the purposes of the Land Registration Acts and will bind a purchaser if coupled with actual occupation.

Facts

Mr Boland was the sole registered proprietor of the matrimonial home. Mrs B had made substantial contributions to the purchase price and she claimed an interest, which had not been entered on the register. Mr Boland later, without the consent of Mrs Boland, mortgaged the property to secure his business debts. The bank made

> no enquiry as to whether Mrs B had any interest in the property, and when Mr B defaulted it sought possession. Mrs B claimed to have an overriding interest which was binding upon the bank.
>
> Held
>
> As a consequence of her equitable interest and actual occupation, Mrs Boland had an overriding interest which the bank had not overreached.

If a mortgage is obtained in order to acquire the property and the beneficial interest is also created on acquisition, the person in actual occupation will usually be deemed to have given implied consent to the mortgage (*Bristol & West Building Society v Henning* [1985]; *Paddington Building Society v Mendelsohn* [1985]; *Abbey National Building Society v Cann* [1991]).

ABBEY NATIONAL BUILDING SOCIETY v CANN [1991]

> **For an overriding interest to be binding, the claimant must be in actual occupation at the date of the disposition.**
>
> Facts
>
> The claimant's furniture was moved into the property prior to completion, whilst she was abroad. She claimed an overriding interest based on actual occupation.
>
> Held
>
> She was not regarded as being in occupation prior to completion. Her claim would only have succeeded if she had been in occupation at the time of disposition and that occupation had been apparent.

If an enforceable charge is redeemed using the proceeds from an unenforceable second charge, the second charge may be enforceable to the value of the first charge (*Equity & Law Home Loans Ltd v Prestidge* [1992]; *Le Foe v Le Foe* [2001]).

If there are two or more trustees, the beneficial interests will be overreached on sale or mortgage (see *City of London Building Society v Flegg* [1988]).

> ### CITY OF LONDON BUILDING SOCIETY v FLEGG [1988]
>
> A conveyance to a purchaser from two trustees or a trust corporation will overreach beneficial interests.
>
> Facts
>
> A property was purchased in the name of a daughter and her husband. The daughter's parents (the Fleggs), also made a financial contribution. The husband later took out a mortgage on the property, but on default, the building society sought possession. The Fleggs claimed an overriding interest in the property because of their contributions to the purchase price and the fact that they were in actual occupation of the property when the mortgage was obtained, and no enquiries were made of them.
>
> Held
>
> An overriding interest was found, but because there were two trustees for sale, the Fleggs' beneficial interest had been overreached on sale in accordance with s 27 of the Law of Property Act 1925.

THE INSURANCE PRINCIPLE – ALTERATION OF THE REGISTER AND INDEMNITY

Alteration/rectification of the register Schedule 4 to the LRA 2002

The Registrar may alter, or the court may order alteration:

> to correct a mistake;
> to bring the register up to date;
> to give effect to a right excepted from first registration.

The Registrar also has power to alter the register:

> To remove a superfluous entry.

Alteration will not be made against a proprietor in possession unless:

> the proprietor has contributed to the mistake by his fraud or lack of care; or
> it would be unjust for the alteration not to be made.

Payment of indemnity

Schedule 8 to the LRA 2002

A person may be indemnified if he has suffered loss because:

- the register has been rectified;
- there is a mistake in an official search or an official copy;
- a document kept at the Land Registry has been lost or destroyed.

No indemnity will be payable if:

- The claimant's loss results wholly from his own lack of care or wholly or partly as a result of the claimant's fraud.

A reduced indemnity may be payable:

- If the claimant's loss results partly from his own lack of care.

You should now be confident that you would be able to tick all the boxes on the checklist at the beginning of this chapter. To check your knowledge of Transferring title to land with registered title why not visit the companion website and take the Multiple Choice Question test. Check your understanding of the terms and vocabulary used in this chapter with the flashcard glossary.

4

Adverse possession and boundaries

Factual possession	☐
Animus possidendi	☐
Adverse possession of land with registered title before 13 October 2003	☐
Adverse possession of land with registered title after 12 October 2003	☐
Adverse possession and leasehold land	☐
Boundaries	☐
Party Wall etc Act 1996	☐

ADVERSE POSSESSION OF LAND WITH UNREGISTERED TITLE

A landowner can usually take action to evict a trespasser or squatter from his land. However, if he delays taking action for 12 years (unregistered land) or 10 years (registered land) he may lose the right to sue because his action will be time barred. This will effectively leave the squatter with superior title to the land.

There are two requirements that the squatter must satisfy (*Powell v McFarlane* [1977]) (refer to table on page 34):

- factual possession of the land for the limitation period; and

- *animus possidendi* (the intention to possess).

▶ POWELL v McFARLANE [1977]

A squatter must establish an appropriate degree of physical control over the land in order to be regarded as being in possession.

Facts

A 14 year old boy grazed his cow on a large open space. He repaired the fence, cut hay and trees, constructed a basic water supply and undertook shooting activities over the land.

Held

The acts were found to amount to temporary enjoyment only. They were insufficient to support a claim for adverse possession as there was no evidence that the boy intended to possess the land for himself. The type of acts that will constitute a sufficient degree of physical control will depend on the nature of the land and the manner in which land of that type is commonly used or enjoyed.

Although the squatter must not acknowledge the title of the paper owner, he may acquire title to the land by adverse possession in the following circumstances:

- When he has been in possession of the property for over 12 years but would have been willing to pay rent to the paper owner, if asked (*Lambeth LBC v Blackburn* [2001]).

ADVERSE POSSESSION AND BOUNDARIES

▶ BUCKINGHAMSHIRE CC v MORAN [1990]

Where the paper owner has a future intention for use of the land this will not prevent a successful claim for adverse possession.

Facts

The squatter fenced off and incorporated land belonging to the Council into his own garden. He later secured it with a lock and chain. The Council argued that the squatter was unable to establish an intention to possess as he knew of the Council's future plans to use the land as part of a road diversion.

Held

The court was satisfied that the squatter had demonstrated an intention to possess in spite of the Council's future plans for the land.

- When he entered the land as a licensee and remained in possession for over 12 years after the expiration of the licence – even though he requested a renewal of the licence (*J A Pye Ltd v Graham* [2001]).

▶ J A PYE (OXFORD) LTD v GRAHAM [2001]

The squatter need only prove intention to possess and not to own the land.

Facts

For several years the defendant had farmed land owned by the claimant under a licence agreement. When the licence expired the claimant refused to grant a new one. The defendant remained in occupation but his subsequent requests for a new licence were ignored. The defendant admitted that he would have been prepared to pay rent if it had been requested.

Held

The defendant succeeded in his claim to adverse possession. He had demonstrated the requisite intention to possess and an intention to own the land was not necessary. His willingness to pay rent did not frustrate his claim.

- When a tenant remained in possession for over 12 years after the expiry of the lease (*Williams v Jones* [2002]).

Factual possession	*Animus possidendi*
'A sufficient degree of exclusive physical control' (Slade J in *Powell v McFarlane* [1977])	'... the intention ... to exclude the world at large, *including the owner with the* paper title ... so far as the process of law will allow' (Slade J in *Powell v McFarlane* [1977])
For a period of 12 years (s 15(1) of the LA 1980)	The squatter only has to intend to 'possess' the land; he does not have to intend to 'own' it (*Buckingham CC v Moran* [1990])
The type of conduct that will indicate factual possession will depend on the facts of the case and the type of land involved (*Red House Farm v Catchpole* [1977])	The squatter may claim adverse possession even though his use of the land is not inconsistent with that of the paper owner (Sched 1 to the LA 1980 and *Moran* [1990])
The rights of successive squatters are cumulative (*Mount Carmel Investments Ltd v Peter Thurlow Ltd* [1988])	The squatter should not acknowledge the paper owner's title: by offering to purchase the land (*Edginton v Clark* [1964]); or by accepting a lease of the land (*Colchester BC v Smith* [1992])
	The limitation period for Crown land is 30 years

ADVERSE POSSESSION OF LAND WITH REGISTERED TITLE BEFORE 13 OCTOBER 2003

Before 13 October 2003 registered land was subject to the 12-year limitation period of the LA 1980 and the rules contained in the LRA 1925. Once the squatter could establish factual possession for a period of 12 years with the necessary *animus possidendi*, he had an overriding interest by virtue of s 70(1)(f) of the LRA 1925. The squatter was entitled to be entered as the proprietor and the paper owner held the property in trust for the squatter pending the latter's registration as the proprietor (s 75 of the LRA 1925). If the squatter is able to establish adverse possession for a period of 12 years, he will be subject to these rules.

In *J A Pye (Oxford) Ltd and J A Pye (Oxford) Land Ltd v the United Kingdom* [2007] the ECHR held that there had been no violation of Article 1 of Protocol No. 1 (protection of property) to the European Convention on Human Rights concerning the applicant companies' loss of ownership of agricultural land through 'adverse possession' to a neighbour who had used the land for more than 12 years without permission.

The Court of Appeal also confirmed in *Ofulue v Bossert* [2008] that the rules on adverse possession did not infringe Convention rights.

> ### ▶ PYE v UK [2007]
>
> **Adverse possession does not breach the right to property as protected under Article 1 of the First Protocol of the European Convention on Human Rights.**
>
> Facts
>
> An appeal was made to the Grand Chamber of the European Court of Human Rights against the earlier first instance decision that adverse possession was in breach of the right to property as protected under Article 1 of the First Protocol of the European Convention on Human Rights.
>
> Held
>
> The Court found by ten votes to seven that there had been no violation of Article 1 of Protocol No. 1 to the Convention.

ADVERSE POSSESSION OF LAND WITH REGISTERED TITLE AFTER 12 OCTOBER 2003

Since 13 October 2003 the rules relating to the adverse possession of registered land are to be found in Sched 6 to the LRA 2002. Schedule 6 provides a new procedure that will make it considerably more difficult to acquire land by adverse possession. Some of the most important changes are as follows:

- No matter how long the duration of his adverse possession, the squatter will not acquire title to the land until he has registered his title.

ADVERSE POSSESSION AND BOUNDARIES

- The squatter may apply to register his title after he has been in adverse possession for a period of 10 years (para 1).
- There is no special limitation period for Crown land, unless that land is foreshore when the limitation period is 60 years (para 13).

The most important changes are outlined below.

> The squatter applies to the Land Registry to be registered as the proprietor of the land

> The Registrar gives notice of the squatter's application to the registered proprietor and anybody else with an interest in the land (para 2). These people will then be given 65 business days to object to the registration of the squatter (para 3 and r 189 of the LRR 2003)

> If there is an objection to the squatter's registration, the objector will have a period of two years to evict the squatter. If there is no objection, the squatter will be registered as the proprietor

> Paragraph 5 provides that the registered proprietor will not be permitted to object if one of three conditions is satisfied:
> - it would be unconscionable because of an equity by estoppel for the applicant to be dispossessed;
> - the applicant is entitled to be registered as the proprietor for some reason other than his adverse possession;
> - in the event of a boundary dispute, the applicant took possession of adjacent land in the reasonable belief that it belonged to him

> If the registered proprietor has objected to the applicant's registration, but has not initiated proceedings to evict him, the applicant may make a further application after a further two years (para 6). The applicant will then be entitled to be registered as the proprietor (para 7)

ADVERSE POSSESSION AND LEASEHOLD LAND

Adverse possession against a tenant does not operate against the landlord's title until the lease comes to an end.

If title to the land is unregistered, the tenant may surrender the lease to the landlord who may then take possession proceedings against the squatter (*Fairweather v St Marylebone Property Trust Ltd* [1963]).

If title to the land is registered, the tenant's surrender will not be effective and the landlord must wait until the term of the lease has ended before gaining possession. This applies whether the squatter has managed to register his title (*Spectrum Investment Co v Holmes* [1981]) or not (*Central London Commercial States Ltd v Kato Kagaku Co Ltd* [1998]).

> ### ▶ FAIRWEATHER v ST MARYLEBONE PROPERTY TRUST LTD [1963]
>
> **For unregistered titles, where a squatter has dispossessed a tenant, the Landlord can recover his land from the squatter if the tenant voluntarily surrenders his lease.**
>
> Facts
>
> A squatter had taken possession of a piece of land for a period in excess of 12 years and was thus entitled to occupy the land for the remainder of the leasehold term.
>
> Held
>
> The court found that once the lease had been surrendered by the tenant the Landlord could legitimately take possession of the land.

THE LAW OF BOUNDARIES

In order to determine the boundary between two plots of land, regard may be had to the following:

- The Land Registry: usually the boundary shown on the register is a general boundary only (s 60 of the LRA 2002). However, it is possible to have the exact boundary recorded (see Pt 10 of the LRR 2003 for the procedure to be followed).

ADVERSE POSSESSION AND BOUNDARIES

- The deeds: very often the parcels clause in the deeds will not be accurate. If the boundaries are clearly established in the deeds, that fact will usually be conclusive (*Woolls v Powling* [1999]; *Burns v Morton* [1999]).

- An informal agreement between the parties to determine a boundary may be enforceable in spite of the fact that it does not comply with s 2 of the LP(MP)A 1989 (*Joyce v Rigolli* [2004]).

- Common law presumptions: the two most frequently encountered are the hedge and ditch presumption (that when plots of land are separated by a hedge and a ditch the presumption is that the boundary is the edge of the ditch farthest from the hedge – *Alan Wibberley Building Ltd v Insley* [1999]) and the *ad medium filum* rule (that, unless there is evidence to the contrary, when the boundary between two plots of land is a road or a river the presumption is that the boundary between the two plots of land runs down the centre of the road or river).

- Adverse possession: when one party has been in possession of the disputed land for the limitation period. If the land is registered and the claimant entered the land as a result of a reasonable mistake, his neighbour will have no opportunity to object to his registration as the proprietor (para 5 of Sched 6 to the LRA 2002).

- Proprietary estoppel: where the owner of disputed land permits an adjoining landowner to act to his detriment on a mistaken belief that he owns the land, the landowner may be estopped from asserting his legal rights.

- Acquiescence: a landowner should not delay in asserting his rights (*Jones v Stones* [1999]).

PARTY WALL ETC ACT 1996

If there is no party wall between adjoining plots of land and one of the landowners wishes to construct one, he may serve notice on the adjoining landowner of his intention to build a wall (s 1). The notice period is one month. If the adjoining landowner agrees, the wall is constructed on the boundary and the expense is shared between the owners. If the adjoining owner does not consent, the wall must be built on the land of the landowner at his own expense.

ADVERSE POSSESSION AND BOUNDARIES

If there is already a party wall, the landowner must serve a 'party structure notice' of two months (s 3) to the adjoining landowner if he intends to strengthen, repair, underpin or demolish it. The adjoining landowner may serve a counter-notice (s 4).

If the adjoining owner does not consent within 14 days, a dispute is deemed to have arisen (s 5).

If any works are undertaken, the landowner must safeguard the adjoining land and, where necessary, pay compensation to the adjoining landowner (s 7).

You should now be confident that you would be able to tick all the boxes on the checklist at the beginning of this chapter. To check your knowledge of Adverse possession and boundaries why not visit the companion website and take the Multiple Choice Question test. Check your understanding of the terms and vocabulary used in this chapter with the flashcard glossary.

5

Trusts of land

- Express trusts
- Statutory trusts
- Implied trusts
- Trusts of land pre-1997
- Trusts of land post-1996
- Powers of the trustees
- Beneficial interests
- Beneficial tenancy in common
- Severance
- Rights of the beneficiaries
- Sale of the trust land
- Termination of a trust of land

WHEN TRUSTS ARISE

EXPRESS TRUSTS

- Expressly created by a settlor, who will appoint trustees, identify the beneficiaries and declare the terms of the trust.

- A declaration of trust of land must be evidenced in writing (s 53(1)(b) of the LPA 1925).

- If title to the land is registered, a restriction may be placed on the register in order to show that a trust exists.

STATUTORY TRUSTS

- Whenever land is conveyed to two or more persons (ss 34–36 of the LPA 1925); when there is an intestacy (s 33 of the AEA 1925); whenever land is conveyed to a minor (s 1(6) of the LPA 1925 and s 1 of TOLATA 1996).

- If title to the land is registered, the registrar is obliged to enter a restriction on the register if he registers two or more persons as the proprietors of a registered estate (s 44 of the LRA 2002).

IMPLIED TRUSTS

- Trusts that are implied in certain circumstances (see resulting and constructive trusts in Chapter 6).

- Resulting and constructive trusts of land do not have to be evidenced in writing (s 53(2) of the LPA 1925).

THE NATURE OF THE TRUST

```
S ⟶    T1   T2
      ─────────────────
      B1   B2   B3   B4
```

In the example above, S (the settlor) has transferred land to two trustees (T1 and T2) to hold for the benefit of four beneficiaries (B1, B2, B3 and B4).

The settlor declares the trust and transfers the property to the trustees. Once he has constituted the trust, by transferring the property, he has no further role to play unless he is also a trustee and/or a beneficiary. A statutory trust will arise automatically if the land is conveyed to two or more people. For example, if land is conveyed to A and B, A and B will hold the land in trust for each other.

The trustees hold the legal estate; they are the legal owners. The names of the trustees will be on the conveyance and, if title to the land is registered, the trustees will be registered at the Land Registry as the proprietors. The trustees do not own the land absolutely: they have a duty to administer the trust for the beneficiaries.

The beneficiaries are the beneficial (or equitable) owners. They are usually entitled to occupy the property and to benefit from any rents and profits arising from the land. They will be entitled to the proceeds if the land is sold. Their interests may be concurrent or successive.

Concurrent interests occur when all of the beneficiaries are entitled to benefit at the same time. For example, if S has transferred land to his trustees to hold for the benefit of his four nephews, this creates concurrent interests, or co-ownership. The beneficiaries are all entitled to benefit from the trust immediately.

If we imagine that B1 is S's wife and B2, B3 and B4 are the children from a previous marriage, S may wish to declare a trust in his will by which he leaves the land to B1 for life with remainder, after B1's death, to B2, B3 and B4. If he does so he creates successive interests. B1 (known as the life tenant) will be entitled to enjoy the property for as long as she lives, and then the other beneficiaries (beneficiaries in remainder) will become entitled to benefit from the land when she dies.

TRUSTS OF LAND BEFORE 1997

There were two types of trusts:

- Strict settlements under the SLA 1925 dealt only with successive interests. The legal estate was held by the tenant for life, who held the land for the beneficiaries in remainder. It has not been possible to create any new strict settlements (s 2 of TOLATA 1996) or entailed interests (Sched 1) since the beginning of 1997. Settlements created before 1997 continue to exist, however.

- Trusts for sale under the LPA 1925 dealt with both successive and concurrent interests. The legal estate was held by the trustees, who held the land for the benefit of the beneficiaries. Sections 4 and 5 of TOLATA 1996 effectively turn all trusts for sale into trusts of land after 1996.

TRUSTS OF LAND AFTER 1996

Since 1 January 1997, it has been possible to create only one type of trust of land. Section 1 of TOLATA 1996 provides that '"trust of land" means ... any trust which consists of or includes land ...'.

THE LEGAL ESTATE

- The legal estate is held by the trustees.
- There must not be more than four trustees (s 34(2) of the LPA 1925 and s 34(2) of the TA 1925).
- If land is conveyed to more than four people and the trustees have not been nominated, the first four named will be the trustees.
- The legal estate is always held as a joint tenancy, with a right of survivorship (*jus accrescendi*).
- The legal joint tenancy can never be severed to form a tenancy in common (s 1(6) and s 36(2) of the LPA 1925).

For example, A, B, C and D hold the legal estate of a plot of land:

| A | B | C | D |

If C dies, A, B and D continue to hold the legal estate:

| A | B | D |

TRUSTS OF LAND AFTER 1996

THE POWERS OF THE TRUSTEES

- The Trustees have all the powers of an absolute owner (s 6(1) of TOLATA 1996).

- The Trustees may partition the land (s 7 of TOLATA 1996).

- The Trustees may delegate any of their functions by power of attorney to any beneficiary of full age who has an interest in the land (s 8 of TOLATA 1996).

- The Trustees may be required by the Trust instrument to obtain consent before exercising any of their powers (s 10 of TOLATA 1996).

- In exercising their functions, trustees must, so far as practicable, consult all of the beneficiaries who are of full age and beneficially entitled to an interest in possession of the land. They should, so far as consistent with the general interest of the trust, give effect to the wishes of the majority (according to the value of their combined interests (s 11 of TOLATA 1996)).

THE BENEFICIAL INTERESTS

Beneficial interests may be held either jointly or in common. Unless there is evidence to the contrary, the presumption will be that 'equity follows the law' [*Stack v Dowden 2007*] and that the beneficial interests are held as a joint tenancy (see *Supperstone v Hurst* [2005]). For example, if land is conveyed to A, B, C, D, E and F, the legal estate will be held by the first four named (s 34(2) of the LPA 1925), but they all have a beneficial interest.

A	B	C	D		

A	B	C	D	E	F

If C dies:

A	B	D		

A	B	D	E	F

45

Where the beneficial interest is held as a joint tenancy, none of the joint tenants have 'shares' in the property. Any attempt by a joint tenant to leave his 'share' of the property by will, will be ineffective (*Campbell v Griffith* [2001]; *Carr v Issard* [2006]).

THE BENEFICIAL TENANCY IN COMMON

Unlike the legal estate, which must be held as a joint tenancy (s 1(6) of the LPA 1925), a beneficial interest may be held in common (otherwise known as an undivided share). Each beneficial tenant in common has his own share of the property and the right of survivorship will not apply. For example:

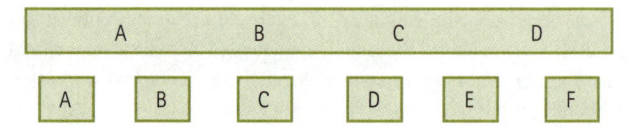

A	B	C	D

A	B	C	D	E	F

If C dies, his share will not be taken by the other tenants in common. C may leave his share to somebody by will, or it will devolve according to the rules of intestacy if he does not make a will. In this case, he has left it to X:

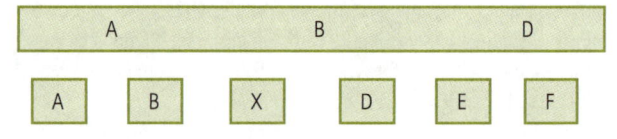

A	B	D

A	B	X	D	E	F

As a tenant in common, C may also sell or give away his share whilst he is still alive. If he does so, he will remain a trustee until he dies or retires from office:

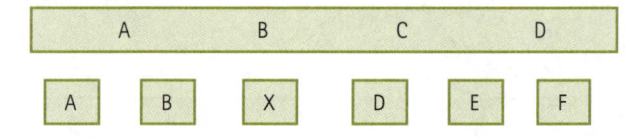

A	B	C	D

A	B	X	D	E	F

CREATION OF A TENANCY IN COMMON

A joint tenancy is characterised by the four unities (*A G Securities v Vaughan* [1990]). If any of the four unities are absent, there cannot be a joint tenancy. The four unities are:

- Unity of possession – all joint tenants must be equally entitled to possession of the land.

- Unity of interest – all joint tenants must have the same interest in the land.

- Unity of time – all joint tenants must have acquired title to the land at the same time.

- Unity of title – each co-owner must claim title under the same document.

A tenancy in common may be created expressly by using 'words of severance' in the conveyance. Examples of words of severance include: 'equally'; 'in equal shares'; 'to be divided between'; 'between'; 'amongst'; 'in equal moieties'. In the example above, the words 'to A, B, C, D, E and F in equal shares' would create a tenancy in common.

Words of severance are unlikely to be conclusive in registered land because the form of transfer (Form TR1) requires transferees to state whether they are to hold the land as joint tenants or as tenants in common.

A tenancy in common will also be presumed in the following circumstances:

- commercial partners who acquire property together (*Lake v Craddock* [1955]);

- purchasers who contribute in unequal shares (*Bull v Bull* [1955]) but see (*Stack v Dowden* [2007]);

- business tenants (*Malayan Credit Ltd v Jack Chia-MPH Ltd* [1986]);

- mortgagees between themselves (*Petty v Styward* [1631]).

Since the case of *Stack v Dowden* [2007], where the interests of co-habitees have not been expressly stated, the existence of joint legal ownership will carry with it a strong presumption of joint beneficial ownership, see also *Fowler v Barron* [2008]. The presumption can be rebutted if one of the co-owners can establish exceptional circumstances. An example would be where the property

TRUSTS OF LAND

had been purchased as an investment (*Lasker v Lasker* [2008], (see also *Ritchie v Ritchie* [2007]).

SEVERANCE

A joint tenant may turn his joint tenancy into a tenancy in common by a process known as severance (s 36(2) of the LPA 1925). In the example below, C has severed his interest, thereby creating a tenancy in common of his share. The others remain as joint tenants:

| A | B | C | D |

| A | B | D | E | F | | C |

Because of the effect of severance, it is not possible to sever a joint tenancy by will – it must take effect *inter vivos*. If it was possible to sever by will, it would be possible for C to defraud his co-owners by agreeing with them to hold the property as a joint tenancy. C could then execute a will that severed the joint tenancy posthumously, thereby defrauding the other co-owners. In such a situation C could not lose: if his co-owners died first, C would obtain their shares by survivorship; but if C died first, the co-owners would find out after his death that they were not to benefit from C's death. The rule against severance by will can have serious implications for solicitors when drafting wills (*Carr-Glynn v Frearsons* [1998]).

METHODS OF SEVERANCE

▶ KINCH v BULLARD [1999]

A severance notice sent by ordinary post will be effective at the time at which the letter would in the ordinary course be delivered, irrespective of whether or not it has been read.

Facts
The husband and wife were Joint Tenants in law and equity. The wife sent a letter to her husband by ordinary post indicating

her wish to sever the Joint Tenancy. Before the letter arrived the husband had a heart attack and was hospitalised. The wife intercepted the letter on the basis that he might die before her and it would no longer be of benefit to her to sever. Both parties died, but the husband died first.

Held
Severance occurred when the letter was delivered. Consequently, under the rules of a tenancy in common the husband's share passed under the terms of his will.

- By written notice (s 36(2) and s 196 of the LPA 1925). The notice must be 'left at' the last known place of abode or business of the other joint tenants (s 196(3)) or may be sent by recorded or special delivery (s 196(4)). A notice sent by ordinary first class post will be sufficient, provided that it is delivered – it has therefore been 'left at' the address, and it does not matter whether the intended recipient actually sees the notice (*Kinch v Bullard* [1999]). A notice sent by recorded delivery will be 'deemed to be made at the time at which the registered letter would in the ordinary course be delivered' (s 196(4) and *WX Investments v Begg* [2002]), and it does not matter whether or not the intended recipient actually receives it (*Re 88 Berkeley Road, London NW9* [1983]).

▶ RE 88 BERKELEY ROAD, LONDON NW9 [1983]

A notice of severance sent by recorded delivery will be effective provided it has not been returned by the post office. This will be the case even when the person who served the notice has signed for its receipt.

Facts
One Joint Tenant served a notice on the other (2nd) Joint Tenant indicating her wish to sever. The Joint Tenant who served the notice also signed for its receipt as the (2nd) Joint Tenant was on holiday. The 2nd Joint Tenant claimed that the severance was not effective, as she had not received the notice.

TRUSTS OF LAND

> Held
> The notice had been correctly served in accordance with s 196(4) LPA 1925 and it was immaterial that the severing party had signed for receipt of the notice.

- By a joint tenant acting upon his own share (selling or mortgaging it – see *First National Securities Ltd v Hegerty* [1985]).

- By mutual agreement (*Burgess v Rawnsley* [1975]).

- By mutual conduct (*Williams v Hensman* [1861]).

- By the bankruptcy of a joint tenant (*Re Dennis* [1995]).

- By merger of interest (one joint tenant acquires the interest of another).

- By forfeiture – when one joint tenant kills another, he may be prohibited from benefiting from his unlawful conduct (*In the Estate of Crippen* [1911]). The forfeiture rule may, in certain circumstances, be modified by the court if the offender is guilty of manslaughter, but not if he is guilty of murder (s 2 of the Forfeiture Act 1982 and *Re K* [1986]).

- By operation of law (for example, the Inheritance (Provision for Family and Dependants) Act 1975).

▶ WILLIAMS v HENSMAN [1861]

> Facts
> Wood V C specified the three methods by which severance will be effective. These are:
> - Operating upon one's own share
> - Mutual agreement
> - Mutual conduct.

▶ BURGESS v RAWNSLEY [1975]

> Severance by mutual agreement will arise where the course of dealings between the parties demonstrates a clear intention that

> land should be held as a Tenancy in Common and not a Joint Tenancy.
>
> Facts
>
> Mr Honick and Mrs Rawnsley formed a relationship and purchased a property as Joint Tenants. The relationship broke down and Mr Honick offered to buy Mrs Rawnsley's share. The parties reached an agreement in principle but had not agreed the price when Mr Honick died.
>
> Held
>
> The COA determined that the Joint Tenancy had been severed and Mr Honick's half share passed to his daughter under his estate.

When a joint tenancy is severed it always severs in equal shares (*Nielson-Jones v Fedden* [1975]). However, if there has been an express declaration regarding shares, the declaration will usually be conclusive (*Goodman v Gallant* [1986]; *Singla v Brown* [2007]). If there is no express declaration, the court may take all of the circumstances of the case into consideration when apportioning shares (*Bernard v Josephs* [1982]).

Section 24 of the Matrimonial Causes Act 1973 gives the court discretion to vary property rights on divorce.

> ▌ GOODMAN v GALLANT [1986]
>
> **Where a conveyance contains an express declaration regarding shares the declaration will be conclusive.**
>
> Facts
>
> Following the breakdown of a relationship, the woman claimed a larger share in the property on account of her larger contributions. The conveyance declared the couple to be Joint Tenants.
>
> Held
>
> The declaration of Joint Tenancy prevailed over the fact that there had been unequal contributions and the couple were awarded equal shares.

RIGHTS OF THE BENEFICIARIES

Section 12(1) of TOLATA 1996 gives the beneficiaries a right to occupy the land provided that their occupation is within the purposes of the trust; and the land is held by the trustees so as to be available.

Section 13 provides that where there are two or more beneficiaries who are entitled to occupy the land, the trustees may allow one or more of them to occupy the land, or part of it, and to restrict the rights of the other beneficiaries (see *Rodway v Landy* [2001]). The trustees must not unreasonably restrict a beneficiary's right of occupation (s 13(2)). A beneficiary in occupation may be required to pay compensation to an excluded beneficiary (s 13(6)). When deciding whether to exercise their powers of exclusion or restriction the trustees are directed to have regard to (s 13(4)):

- the intention of the person (if any) who created the trust;
- the purposes for which the property is held;
- the circumstances and wishes of each of the beneficiaries who is entitled to occupy the land.

SALE OF THE TRUST LAND

The interests of the beneficiaries are overreached on sale provided that the capital money is paid to, and a receipt obtained from, the trustees, being at least two in number or a trust corporation (ss 2 and 27 of the LPA 1925).

Section 14 of TOLATA 1996 provides that any person interested (trustee, beneficiary, mortgagee, etc) may apply to the court for an order:

- relating to the exercise by trustees of any of their functions (including the exercise of their power of sale); or
- declaring the nature or extent of a person's interest under the trust.

Very often the dispute will arise when one or more of the persons interested wants to sell the land but others do not. Under s 14, the court may make 'such order as the court thinks fit'.

When determining an application for an order under s 14, the matters to which the court is to have regard include those listed in s 15:

- the intentions of the person or persons who created the trust (s 15(1)(a));

- the purposes for which the property is held (s 15(1)(b));

- the welfare of any minor who occupies or might reasonably be expected to occupy the property as his home (s 15(1)(c)). The court will require specific evidence on how a child's welfare will be affected if an order of sale is granted (*First National Bank plc v Achampong* [2003]);

- the interests of any secured creditor of any beneficiary (s 15(1)(d));

- the circumstances and wishes of any beneficiaries of full age and entitled to an interest in possession or, in the case of dispute, to the majority (according to their combined interests) (s 15(3)).

Before 1997 (when applications were brought under s 30 of the LPA 1925), there was presumption in favour of sale but the courts would not order sale when there was a collateral purpose (*Re Buchanan-Wollaston's Conveyance* [1939]; *Abbey National plc v Moss* [1994]) until that purpose had ended (*Jones v Challenger* [1961]; *Bank of Ireland Home Mortgages Ltd v Bell* [2001]). Since TOLATA came into force, there has been no presumption in favour of sale, and the old cases, though often useful, 'should be treated with caution' (*Mortgage Corp Ltd v Shaire* [2001]).

> ### ▶ RE BUCHANAN-WOLLASTON'S CONVEYANCE [1939]
>
> Under a trust for sale an application for sale of co-owned land could be refused where the main purpose of the trust still existed.
>
> Facts
>
> Four home owners purchased a piece of land to prevent development which would obstruct their view of the sea. It was agreed that the land would only be sold if there was unanimous consent. One of the owners later wished to sell his property and made an application to the court for the sale of the co-owned land.
>
> Held
>
> An order of sale was refused since the purpose of the trust still existed.

Section 15 does not apply in insolvency, which is governed by s 335A of the Insolvency Act 1986. After one year of the bankrupt's estate vesting in the trustee in bankruptcy, the court is directed to assume that the interests of the bankrupt's creditors outweigh all other considerations, unless the circumstances of the case are exceptional. Examples of cases involving exceptional circumstances are *Re Holliday* [1981] and *Claughton v Charalambous* [1998].

In *Barca v Mears* [2004] it was contended that an order of sale after 12 months may contravene Article 8 ECHR, but there has been a lack of support for this argument in later cases (*Nicholls v Lan* [2006]).

TERMINATION OF A TRUST OF LAND
This occurs:

- when the land is sold;
- when one beneficiary acquires the entire beneficial interest. This may occur by survivorship or by one beneficiary purchasing the shares of the other beneficiaries;
- by partition of the land. Each beneficiary will receive his own deeds (unregistered land) or registered title (registered land).

You should now be confident that you would be able to tick all the boxes on the checklist at the beginning of this chapter. To check your knowledge of Trusts of land why not visit the companion website and take the Multiple Choice Question test. Check your understanding of the terms and vocabulary used in this chapter with the flashcard glossary.

6

Resulting trusts, constructive trusts, proprietary estoppel and licences

Resulting trusts

Constructive trusts

Overreaching an interest in land subject to resulting or constructive trusts

Proprietary estoppel

Comparison of rights

Licences

A declaration of trust of land should be evidenced in writing (s 53(1)(b) of the LPA 1925). However, it is possible to acquire an interest in land without any formalities by way of resulting or constructive trusts (s 53(2)) or by way of proprietary estoppel.

RESULTING TRUSTS

A resulting trust of land arises by way of presumption. The presumption is raised by contributions towards the purchase price of the land. Contributions made by way of mortgage loan may give rise to the presumption, but, since *Curley v Parkes* [2004], it appears that mortgage repayments which are made after acquisition may give rise to a constructive, rather than a resulting, trust.

A right-to-buy discount may count as a contribution (*Springette v Defoe* [1992]). The presumption may be rebutted if the contributions were intended to be a gift or a loan.

The presumption of advancement (that contributions from husband to wife or from father to child are presumed to be gifts) may also apply. However, the current status of the presumption of advancement is questionable (see *Pettitt v Pettitt* [1970]). A beneficiary under a resulting trust has an interest in the land in proportion to his contributions.

CONSTRUCTIVE TRUSTS

Anybody claiming an interest in land by way of constructive trust must satisfy three requirements (*Lloyds Bank plc v Rosset* [1991]):

- a common intention that they were to benefit;
- detrimental reliance upon the common intention;
- unconscionability or equitable fraud on the part of the legal owner.

CONSTRUCTIVE TRUSTS

> ### LLOYDS BANK PLC v ROSSET [1991]
>
> **In determining whether an individual has a beneficial interest in the family home the court will look for evidence of common intention and detrimental reliance.**
>
> Facts
>
> Mr and Mrs Rosset purchased a run-down property which required substantial renovation work. Mrs Rosset spent considerable time supervising the works and completed some of the decoration herself. Mr Rosset was working abroad for the majority of this time. The marriage broke down and Mrs Rosset claimed a beneficial interest in the property based on the work that she had undertaken.
>
> Held
>
> Mrs Rosset's claim failed as the court was unable to find a common intention that she would acquire a share in the property.

A beneficiary under a constructive trust of land has an interest in the land. The court may take into account all the circumstances of a case when quantifying the extent of that interest – a 'broad brush' approach (*Drake v Whipp* [1995]; *Oxley v Hiscock* [2004]).

> ### DRAKE v WHIPP [1995]
>
> **In assessing the relative shares under a resulting or constructive trust, once a common intention has been established the court may take a broad approach to quantification of the shares. This will include both direct financial and non-financial contributions.**
>
> Facts
>
> The parties purchased a property together and the legal title was registered solely in the man's name. The woman's contribution to the purchase and conversion costs equated to around 20% of the property's value. There was a common intention between the parties that they would share the property.

> **Held**
>
> The court considered all relevant factors and awarded the woman a one-third share in the property.

The 'broad brush' approach to quantification has been used when the claimant appears to have acquired an interest by way of *resulting* trust (*Midland Bank v Cooke* [1995]; *Le Foe v Le Foe* [2001]; *Oxley v Hiscock* [2004]).

Where a property has been transferred in joint names and there has been no statement as to how the beneficial interests are held, the court will follow the approach taken in *Oxley* as to the calculation of beneficial interests, but will base the calculations on the intentions of the parties, rather than on what is fair (*Stack v Dowden* [2007]).

▶ STACK v DOWDEN [2007]

Where a property is purchased in joint names and there is no express agreement about the parties' shares in the property, in family cases, there will be a strong presumption of joint beneficial ownership, except for in exceptional cases. The aim of the court is to ascertain the parties' shared intentions in the light of their whole course of conduct.

Facts

The parties had co-habited since 1983; they had four children; and the relationship ended in October 2002. The property in dispute was purchased in August 1993 and registered in joint names. The purchase price for the property was provided partly by a mortgage in joint names and partly from funds generated by the woman, from the sale of her own previous property and from her savings. There was no express declaration of the beneficial interests. The man sought a declaration that the property was held by the parties on trust for themselves as tenants in common in equal shares.

Held

The HOL held that this was an 'exceptional case', the facts of which displaced the assumption of joint tenancy. Mrs Dowden was

CONSTRUCTIVE TRUSTS

> awarded a 65 per cent share, and Mr Stack 35 per cent based upon the court's findings of fact as to their intentions.

Later in *Fowler v Barron* [2008], the COA found an absence of 'exceptional' circumstances to justify a departure from the earlier rule (*Stack v Dowden* [2007]).

A constructive trust of land may also arise when one party acquires land from another expressly 'subject to' a prior agreement (*Binions v Evans* [1972]; *Lyus v Prowsa Developments Ltd* [1982]).

A common intention may be established or evidenced by:

- evidence of an express agreement; or

- contributions after the acquisition of the property (*Hussey v Palmer* [1972]), or perhaps even at the time of acquisition (*Oxley v Hiscock* [2004]). The contributions must be referable to the realty (*Burns v Burns* [1984]), but contributions by themselves are not sufficient – they must evidence a common intention (*Thomas v Fuller-Brown* [1988]);

- 'regular substantial mortgage repayments' (Lord Diplock in *Gissing v Gissing* [1971]; *Curley v Parkes* [2004]; or

- an 'express promise' by the legal owner – *Eves v Eves* [1975] (assurance by a man that the house would be in joint names if his partner was 21); *Grant v Edwards* [1986] (excuse made by man that the woman's name had to be kept off the title deeds to prevent her husband obtaining an interest in the property on divorce); *Hammond v Mitchell* [1991] ('when we are married the house will be half yours anyway').

▶ EVES v EVES [1975]

Acquisition of a beneficial interest will arise where a party has been led to believe that they would acquire a beneficial interest, even if the other party had other unstated intentions.

Facts

The couple were co-habiting in a property vested solely in the man's name. He had told her that she was not old enough to have a legal estate in the property. The woman had made no financial contributions, but had undertaken substantial renovation work on the property. The woman claimed a beneficial interest in the property.

Held

The court found the discussions to be sufficient evidence of a common intention and the woman was awarded a share in the property under a constructive trust.

GRANT v EDWARDS [1986]

Where there is a clear inference from discussions as to why one of the parties' names has not been put on the legal title, a beneficial interest will be recognised where that party believed they were to acquire an interest.

Facts

The parties had discussed the woman's interest in the property in which they were co-habiting. The man informed her that he had left her name off the legal title because it may have affected her divorce settlement. He later denied her interest.

Held

The court found a clear inference from the parties' discussions that the woman was to have a beneficial interest in the property.

PURCHASE OF LAND SUBJECT TO RESULTING OR CONSTRUCTIVE TRUSTS

A purchaser of the legal estate will take the land free from interests under a trust provided that he obtains a receipt from the trustees, being at least two in number or a trust corporation (ss 2 and 27 of the LPA 1925; *City of London Building Society v Flegg* [1988]).

If the land is unregistered, a non-overreachable interest will bind a purchaser if he has notice, actual or constructive, of that interest (*Kingsnorth Finance Co Ltd v Tizard* [1986]).

If title to the land is registered, a non-overreachable interest will bind a purchaser if the owner of the interest is in actual occupation of the land and the circumstances satisfy the requirements of para 2 of Sched 3 (or Sched 1 if the land is subject to first registration) to the LRA 2002.

Overreaching may also occur in circumstances where no monetary exchange has taken place, provided that a sum of money is payable. In *State Bank of India v Sood* [1997], overreaching occurred when the trustees mortgaged a property in return for an overdraft facility.

PROPRIETARY ESTOPPEL

The modern definition of proprietary estoppel was given by Lord Oliver in *Taylor's Fashions Ltd v Liverpool Victoria Trustees Co Ltd* [1982]. An equity by estoppel will arise when it would be 'unconscionable for a party to be permitted to deny that which, knowingly or unknowingly, he has allowed another to assume to his detriment'. The test is therefore one of unconscionability which will arise when the following factors are present:

- promise, assurance, representation or acquiescence on the part of the legal owner;
- detriment;
- reliance.

The elements of reliance and detriment are often intertwined and the court is to 'look at the matter in the round' (*Gillett v Holt* [2000]). The category of acceptable 'detrimental' acts is fairly wide, but the act must be something substantial. In *Jennings v Rice* [2002], the claimant worked unpaid for several years; in *Yaxley v Gotts* [2000], the claimant undertook conversion and refurbished work on a property based upon a promise that he would be given one of the flats contained within. Having established promise and detriment, it must be determined whether it would be unconscionable to allow the promisor to go back on his promise. There should be a broad analysis of the facts which give rise to the unconscionability (*Gillet v Holt*).

The remedy awarded to a successful claimant will be 'the minimum equity to do justice' (*Baker v Baker* [1993]): it may amount to a freehold estate in the land (*Pascoe v Turner* [1979]); a right to occupy a property for life (*Greasley v Cooke* [1980]); a right of access (*Crabb v Arun DC* [1976]); or a right of way (*ER Ives v High* [1967]).

RESULTING TRUSTS, CONSTRUCTIVE TRUSTS, PROPRIETARY ESTOPPEL AND LICENCES

▶ PASCOE v TURNER [1979]

Where a claimant has relied upon a representation to his detriment the court will determine the interest as promised.

Facts

Mrs Turner entered the household as a housekeeper. Later she entered into a relationship with Mr Pascoe and he told her that she could consider the house and its contents as hers. Mr Pascoe later denied that Mrs Turner had any right to the house.

Held

The court found that Mrs Turner had relied upon a representation to her detriment and ordered that the freehold of the property be transferred to her.

The role of unconscionability was re-examined in *Cobbe v Yeoman's Row Management* [2008]. Whilst unconscionability plays an important role in estoppel, it must be accompanied by the other key elements, assurance, detriment and reliance.

▶ COBBE v YEOMAN'S ROW MANAGEMENT LTD [2008]

HOL drew a distinction between domestic and commercial cases in estoppel. A claim to estoppel will not succeed where an agreement has been made 'subject to contract'.

Facts

An agreement to purchase some land was made between C and YRM. Both parties knew that the agreement was not a legally binding contract. C wanted to develop the site and spent a substantial amount of time and money in the acquisition of planning permission. Once granted, YRM refused to complete the sale.

Held

HOL refused the claim for estoppel. The expectation created from the agreement was speculative and both parties knew that the agreement was not legally binding.

▶ GILLETT v HOLT [2000]

An estoppel interest can be acquired where the promise relied upon is a revocable act.

Facts
A close social and business relationship existed between the parties, and the defendant relied upon the claimant. Over a period of years the claimant was publicly assured by the defendant that he would become the owner of the defendant's estate upon his death. In reliance on these assurances, the claimant invested in the defendant's business throughout his life. The relationship later broke down and the defendant no longer relied upon the claimant.

Held
The estoppel claim was upheld. The claimant had relied upon a promise to his detriment. The fact that the will could be revoked at a later date was immaterial.

Section 116 of the LRA 2002 confirms that, in relation to registered land, an equity by estoppel is capable of binding successors in title. The claimant may therefore enter his interest as a notice at the Land Registry or, if in actual occupation, claim an overriding interest. The status of the right in unregistered land depends upon the doctrine of notice (*ER Ives v High* [1967]).

THE RIGHTS COMPARED

Resulting trust	Constructive trust	Proprietary estoppel
Requires: Presumption raised by a contribution made at the time of acquisition The presumption may be rebutted if the contribution was a gift or a loan	*Requires*: Common intention Reliance Detriment Unconscionability	*Requires*: Assurance, representation or acquiescence Reliance Detriment Unconscionability

(*Continued*)

Resulting trust	Constructive trust	Proprietary estoppel
Remedy: An interest in proportion to the contribution	*Remedy*: The 'broad brush' approach Look at the intention of the parties	*Remedy*: The minimum equity to do justice

Since *Oxley v Hiscock* [2004] it appears that the courts will look for evidence of a common intention in order to find a constructive trust, even if the evidence of the constructive trust is to be found in contributions made at the time of acquisition. The resulting trust will therefore only be relevant if it is not possible to infer a common intention from such contributions (see *Curley v Parkes* [2004]).

There are obvious similarities between constructive trusts and proprietary estoppel and it has long since been recognised that in some circumstances an interest could arise by either method (see *Grant v Edwards* [1986]). More controversially, in *Oxley v Hiscock* [2004], Chadwick LJ considered that in cohabitation cases there is little, if any, difference in outcome between constructive trusts and proprietary estoppel.

LICENCES

A licence is merely a permission to do something on the land or to occupy it. It is not an interest in the land, even if it involves occupation of land for many years.

Licences may be divided into four categories:

Bare licence

A bare licence is a mere permission to do something on land which, without permission, would be a trespass. A typical example occurs when a landowner permits a child to retrieve a lost ball from his garden.

A bare licence may be revoked at will.

Licence coupled with an interest

Typically, the interest will be a contractual right or a profit *à prendre*. For example, if a landowner makes a contract with somebody to cut and take away timber from his land (*James Jones Ltd v Earl of Tankerville* [1909]), or grants him a profit of estovers (right to take wood), he must be impliedly granting him a licence to enter his land in order to exercise the benefit of the contract or profit.

In this case, the licence will usually be irrevocable throughout the period of the grant or contractual term.

Contractual licence

A contractual licence is simply a licence that has been granted by valid contract. Termination of the licence is only possible within the terms of the contract. If there is no express provision in the contract, reasonable notice must be given to terminate the licence (*Winter Garden Theatre Ltd v Millennium Productions Ltd* [1948]). A contractual licence generally does not bind third parties (*King v David Allen Ltd* [1916], but see also *Errington v Errington and Woods* [1952]).

A contractual licence is not an interest in the land and cannot be an overriding interest (*Ashburn Anstalt v Arnold* [1989]).

Estoppel licence

An estoppel licence is a licence that has been acquired by proprietary estoppel (see above for proprietary estoppel).

You should now be confident that you would be able to tick all the boxes on the checklist at the beginning of this chapter. To check your knowledge of Resulting trusts, constructive trusts, proprietary estoppel and licences why not visit the companion website and take the Multiple Choice Question test. Check your understanding of the terms and vocabulary used in this chapter with the flashcard glossary.

7

Leases

Concept of a lease	☐
Creation of leases and formalities	☐
Protection of a lease	☐
Essential requirements of a lease	☐
Lease/licence distinction	☐
Social housing	☐
Leasehold covenants	☐
Enforcement of covenants pre-1 January 1996	☐
Enforcement of covenants post-31 December 1995	☐
Landlord's remedies for breach of covenant	☐
Tenant's remedies for breach of covenant	☐
Methods of terminating leases	☐

A lease is also known as a term of years, a demise or a tenancy. Whatever term is used, it is the second legal estate in land (s 1(1) of the LPA 1925).

THE CONCEPT OF THE LEASE

Section 205(1)(xxvii) of the LPA 1925 defines a lease. It is an estate in the land for a fixed maximum term, which may be of any duration from one week (or even less) to 3,000 years (or even more). Typically, a long lease will be granted by a landlord (lessor) to a tenant (lessee) who will pay a lump sum (or premium) and a small amount of periodic rent (eg, it may be as little as a peppercorn annually). Short leases may not involve the payment of a premium, but will usually involve the payment of rent periodically.

TERMINOLOGY

Term	Example
Leases: in this example, A, the freeholder, has granted a lease for 999 years to B. B and his successors will go into possession of the land for 999 years, after which time the lease will determine (terminate). After 999 years, A's successor will be able to recover possession. The landlord is said to hold the reversion because the property will revert back to him when the lease ends.	**A** Landlord (freehold estate) ↓ (999 years) **B** Tenant (leasehold estate)
Subleases: in this example, A has granted a lease for a term of 999 years to B, who sublets the property to C for 99 years, who sublets to D for 9 years. A sublease may be of any period provided that it is shorter than the superior lease by at least one day. A is the landlord of the head lease (the superior lease) and D is the tenant under the final sublease. B is the tenant under the 999-year lease and the landlord of the 99-year lease. Similarly, C is the tenant under the 99-year lease and the landlord of the 9-year lease.	**A** The lessor or landlord ↓ (999 years) **B** A's tenant –also C's landlord ↓ (99 years) **C** B's tenant –also D's landlord ↓ (9 years) **D** The sublessee or subtenant

> Assignments: in contrast to a sublease, an assignment occurs when the whole of an interest is transferred. In this case, A has granted a 999-year lease to B and has then assigned his reversion to Y, who is now the landlord. B has also assigned the lease to X, who is now the tenant.
>
> A → Y (assignment of the reversion)
>
> ↓ (999 years)
>
> B → X (assignment of the lease)

TYPES OF LEASE

Assignments: in contrast to a sublease, an assignment occurs when the whole of an interest is transferred. In this case, A has granted a 999-year lease to B and has then assigned his reversion to Y, who is now the landlord. B has also assigned the lease to X, who is now the tenant.

A → Y (assignment of the reversion)
↓ (999 years)
B → X (assignment of the lease)

Fixed term leases: the lease is granted for a fixed period (1,000 years, 10 years, etc). The lease will determine when the period comes to an end.

Yearly tenancies: yearly tenancies may be created expressly or by the tenant going into possession and paying rent calculated by reference to a year. The lease continues from year to year until notice is given. Unless agreed to the contrary, the notice period is usually six months.

Legal periodic tenancies: legal periodic tenancies may be created either expressly or by the tenant going into possession and offering rent. If no term is specified, the term will be the period by which rent is calculated – for example, rent of £1,200 per year, payable monthly, creates a yearly, rather than a monthly, tenancy. If no term is agreed but rent has been offered and accepted, the term will be one rental period. Legal periodic tenancies determine when one party serves a notice to quit. In the absence of a contrary agreement, the notice period should be one full term. Residential tenants should generally be given at least four weeks' notice (s 5 of the PEA 1977) unless they are excluded tenants under the HA 1988 and they have agreed to the contrary with the landlord. The tenant will often enjoy some form of statutory protection.

Tenancies at will: tenancies at will arise when a tenant occupies land as a tenant subject to an agreement with the landlord that either party may determine the tenancy at any time. A classic example of a tenancy at will occurs when a landlord permits a tenant into occupation whilst negotiations for an agreement are proceeding (see *Javad v Aqil* [1991]). The status of a tenancy at will is uncertain: the tenant has no estate in the land and his rights are more akin to those of a licensee.

Tenancies at sufferance: tenancies at sufferance occur when a tenant, without the landlord's consent or dissent, holds over at the end of a leasehold term. A tenant at sufferance is not a trespasser (he entered the land with permission), nor is he a tenant (his tenancy has ceased); his status is more akin to a squatter. If the landlord assents to his occupation, the tenant at sufferance will become a tenant at will.

CREATION OF LEASES AND STATUTORY FORMALITIES

Legal leases

- *Term over three years*: must be made by deed (s 52(1) of the LPA 1925).

- *Three years or less*: may be created by parol (s 54(2) of the LPA 1925).

- *A lease over 7 years (post LRA 2002)* requires a deed and registration to be legal.

- *Assignments of leases*: must be made by deed regardless of the term. (*Crago v Julien* [1992]).

Equitable leases

Require a valid contract: s 2 of the LP(MP)A 1989.

Such a lease is known as a lease under the rule in *Walsh v Lonsdale* [1882]. It is not really a lease: it is a contract to create a lease, but equity reads the agreement as a lease because 'equity sees as done that which ought to be done' and may grant specific performance of the contract.

WALSH v LONSDALE [1882]

A lease for over three years which has not been created by deed may form a valid equitable lease provided that it satisfies the requirements set out in s 2 Law of Property (Miscellaneous Provisions) Act 1989.

Facts

An agreement to lease a mill had been executed in writing but not by deed. The rent was payable annually in advance and would vary depending upon the success of the business. The tenant went into occupation and paid the rent at the end of each six month period, which the Landlord accepted for 18 months. After this period and without notice the Landlord demanded the rent in advance in line with the original agreement. A challenge then arose as to whether or not there was a valid lease.

Held

The courts accepted that a valid equitable lease existed, on the basis that 'equity looks on that which ought to be done'. The parties had intended to create a lease and equity assumed that they had done so.

Tenancies by estoppel

When a landlord and tenant have purported to create a valid lease, the landlord may not deny the title of the tenant and the tenant may not deny the title of his landlord. If the landlord did not have the legal estate when he purportedly granted the lease but he subsequently acquires it, the estoppel is said to have been 'fed' and the tenant will acquire a lease as soon as the landlord acquires the estate.

Tenancies acquired by proprietary estoppel

A lease may be created without formalities when the tenant has acted to his detriment in reliance upon a promise or representation which has been made to him by the landowner (see *Yaxley v Gotts* [2000]).

PROTECTION OF THE LEASE

PROTECTION OF THE LEASE AGAINST PURCHASERS

Registered land

Legal leases over seven years and assignments with more than seven years left to run: these are registrable estates at the Land Registry (s 4 of the LRA 2002). Before 13 October 2003, the qualifying period was 21 years.

Legal leases for seven years or less: these are overriding interests (para 1 to Scheds 1 and 3 to the LRA 2002).

Equitable leases: these should be entered as a notice against the lessor's title, though they may be overriding interests if the lessee remains in actual occupation (para 2 of Scheds 1 and 3 to the LRA 2002).

Unregistered land

Legal leases: these are rights *in rem* which do not require protection.

Equitable leases: these should be entered as estate contracts (Class C(iv) land charge) in the Land Charges Register (s 2(4) of the LCA 1972).

STATUTORY PROTECTION FOR PERIODIC TENANTS

Because periodic tenants depend on renewal of their tenancies, their status is rather precarious. The landlord may evict them at common law by serving a valid notice to quit. Some tenants may be able to claim statutory protection:

Business tenants may be able to claim the protection of Part II of the Landlord and Tenant Act 1954. The Act provides for limited security of tenure, and may be excluded.

Agricultural tenants may be subject to the Agricultural Holdings Act 1986 or the Agricultural Tenancies Act 1995. Both Acts provide limited security of tenure.

Residential tenants may be subject to one of the following:

- The Rent Act 1977 (protected tenancies) applies to private residential tenancies created before 15 January 1989. The landlord needs adequate grounds to evict the tenant, who also has the benefit of rent control.

- The Housing Act 1985 (secure tenancies) provides security of tenure to public sector tenants.

- The Housing Act 1988 (assured tenancies) applies to private residential tenancies created after 14 January 1989. In its original form the 1988 Act curtailed the statutory scheme of the 1977 Act and introduced the assured shorthold tenancy, which enabled the landlord to recover possession easily and quickly. Since the Housing Act 1996, all tenancies take effect as shortholds unless the parties expressly choose to create an assured tenancy.

ESSENTIAL REQUIREMENTS FOR A LEASE

▶ STREET v MOUNTFORD [1985]

An agreement will create a tenancy if it is for a term certain, at a rent, with exclusive possession unless there are exceptional circumstances which will render it a licence.

Facts

Mrs Mountford signed an agreement termed a 'licence'. However the document had all of the key features usually found in a tenancy, including the right to exclusive possession of the premises. Mrs Mountford later claimed protection under the Rent Acts which did not protect a licensee.

Held

The court found that a tenancy had been created regardless of the fact that the agreement was termed a licence, since it had all of the key features of a tenancy.

In addition to the formality and registration requirements, a lease has certain distinguishing characteristics. These were identified by Lord Templeman in *Street v Mountford* [1985] as being 'exclusive possession for a fixed or periodic term certain in consideration of a premium or periodic payments'. In other words the three requirements are: exclusive possession; for a term certain; at a rent or premium. To deal with the requirements in reverse order:

Rent or premium

Section 205(1)(xxvii) defines a lease as taking effect 'whether or not at a rent' and it is possible to create a rent-free lease (see *Ashburn Anstalt v Arnold* [1989] and *Ingram v IRC* [1999]). However, the absence of rent usually indicates that the occupier occupies the property as a licensee rather than as a tenant.

If rent is paid, it must be a fixed sum and not a fluctuating amount (*Bostock v Bryant* [1990]).

Term certain

A lease must have a fixed maximum duration. The agreement may contain a break clause (eg, a 20-year lease with an option to determine every five years) or a provision that determines the lease upon the happening of a particular event, but the maximum duration must be known at the outset. For this reason there could not be a lease when property was let 'for the duration' of the war in *Lace v Chantler* [1944]. In *Prudential Assurance Co v London Residuary Body* [1992], there was held to be no lease until Walworth Road was required for widening, but the tenant was deemed to have a yearly tenancy because rent had been offered and accepted on that basis.

▶ LACE v CHANTLER [1944]

A lease will not take effect unless it is possible to ascertain its duration from the start.

Facts

A lease was granted during the Second World War, stating the period to be 'for the duration of the war'.

Held

The lease was invalid as the duration of the war was unknown and could not constitute a 'term certain'.

Exclusive possession

The occupier must have control over the property (*National Car Parks Ltd v Trinity Development Co Ltd* [2001]) and must be able to exclude the landlord.

PROTECTION OF THE LEASE

Certain categories of people will not be tenants even if they have exclusive occupation of the property. Such categories include:

- Tenants at will;

- Tenants at sufferance;

- Tolerated trespassers – when a public sector landlord permits an ex-tenant to remain in occupation even though a possession order has been made against the ex-tenant, the ex-tenant remains in occupation as a tolerated trespasser (*Stirling v Leadenhall Residential 2 Ltd* [2001]; he does not become tenant even if he pays rent and it is accepted (*Newham LBC v Hawkins* [2005]) unless the landlord offers a new tenancy agreement (*Swindon BC v Aston* [2002]);

- Service occupiers who occupy for the better performance of their duties (*Norris v Checksfield* [1991] – coach mechanic and chauffeur; *Surrey CC v Lamond* [1998] – school caretaker);

▶ NORRIS v CHECKSFIELD [1991]

Where an employer allows an employee to live in accommodation which has been provided to ensure that he is readily available for work at any time, the employee may be regarded as a service occupier, which affords only the status of licensee.

Facts
A coach mechanic was granted the use of a bungalow close to the depot. The employer argued that the agreement was a service occupancy not a tenancy.

Held
The court found that the agreement constituted a service occupancy affording the employee the status of a licensee only.

- Occupation based on acts of charity, generosity or friendship (*Facchini v Bryson* [1952]; *Marcroft Wagons Ltd v Smith* [1951]; *Gray v Taylor* [1998]);

- Occupiers who have services provided for them (*Otter v Norman* [1989] – a continental breakfast);

- Lodgers – people with a resident landlord (*Street v Mountford* [1985]; *Mortgage Corp Ltd v Ubah* [1997]).

MARCROFT WAGONS LTD v SMITH [1951]

Occupation based on an act of kindness will constitute a licence.

Facts

The landlord, out of genuine kindness, allowed the daughter of deceased tenants to remain in occupation for a period following a double bereavement. The daughter later contended that she had been granted a tenancy.

Held

The Court rejected the daughter's claim, refusing to impose upon the landlord the statutory obligations of the Rent Acts in return for his act of kindness.

FACCHINI v BRYSON [1952]

Where the circumstances of an agreement constitute a family arrangement, act of friendship or generosity, a licence will be favoured over a tenancy.

Facts

An employer and his assistant entered into an agreement which allowed the assistant to occupy a property for a weekly payment with exclusive possession.

Held

The assistant was held to be a service occupier. The judge provided guidance on the criteria to establish between a licence and a tenancy in less formal circumstances.

THE LEASE/LICENCE DISTINCTION

Because of the protection given to tenants by the RA 1977, landlords attempted to evade the RA, which applied only to tenancies, by purporting to

PROTECTION OF THE LEASE

grant licences instead of leases. Landlords sought to grant licences by denying exclusive possession to occupiers.

The distinction is less important for tenancies created since the HA 1988 because landlords are now able to recover possession at the end of the term by granting assured shorthold tenancies. Nevertheless, the cases that came before the courts on the RA 1977 have provided our modern definition of a lease:

- *Somma v Hazelhurst and Savelli* [1978]: the landlord was deemed to be able to grant a licence to two occupiers simply by calling the agreement a licence. The fact that the agreement included a sham clause allowing the licensor or anybody nominated by him to share with the couple was deemed to be irrelevant.

- *Street v Mountford* [1985]: the House of Lords overruled *Somma*. Lord Templeman stated that if a landlord grants exclusive possession, for a term certain, at a rent or premium, he has created a lease, notwithstanding the fact that the agreement is termed a licence. The court should 'be astute to frustrate sham devices and artificial transactions whose only object is to disguise the grant of a tenancy and to evade the Rent Acts' (see also *Aslan v Murphy* [1990] – the landlord kept a key and denied possession to the tenant between the hours of 10.30 and 12 noon each day).

When there is more than one occupant, the issue is one of fact, depending upon the nature of the accommodation and the relationship between the occupiers (*Stribling v Wickham* [1989]). As a rough rule of thumb, if the occupiers are jointly liable for the whole of the rent a joint tenancy (lease) exists; if the occupants are liable only for their 'share' of the rent they are probably licensees (*Mikeover v Brady* [1989]). The House of Lords decided in *A G Securities v Vaughan* [1990] that, in order for a joint tenancy to exist, the four unities must be present: unity of possession, interest, time and title. In *Vaughan*, Lord Oliver found that none of the unities was present and that 'each person is individually liable for his own rent, which may differ in practice from the amounts paid by all or one of the others . . . '.

In *Antoniades v Villiers* [1992], the House of Lords decided that two occupants of a bed-sitting room were tenants despite the fact that they were, in theory, each liable for their own rent. As Lord Oliver explained, the presumption as to rent 'rest[s] upon the assumption that the licences are not sham documents, which is the very question in issue'.

One successful method used by landlords to avoid the Rent Acts is letting only to a company. Company lets are subject to Pt II of the LTA 1954, rather than the RA 1977 (*Hilton v Plustitle* [1988]; *Eaton Square Properties Ltd v O'Higgins* [2000]).

SOCIAL HOUSING

There have been a number of decisions in recent years concerning tenancies or licences of social housing. They include:

- *Family Housing Association v Jones* [1990]: provision of temporary accommodation at less than market rent created a tenancy.

- *Westminster CC v Clarke* [1992]: the House of Lords held that an occupant of a bedsit in a hostel for single homeless men, who could be moved to another room without notice, was a licensee.

- *Gray v Taylor* [1998]: an occupant of almshouses who paid towards her upkeep was held to be a licensee.

- *Bruton v London and Quadrant Housing Trust* [1999]: the House of Lords held that an occupant of temporary housing for the homeless was a tenant for the purposes of s 11 of the LTA 1985 in spite of the fact that the 'landlord' was only a licensee. If the grantor did not have a legal estate in the land, how is it possible for him to grant a lease to the grantee (*nemo dat quod non habet*)? Lord Hoffmann decided that the occupant was a tenant because he had exclusive possession for a term at a rent, but that his lease would not bind third parties. The decision appears to create a new type of interest – a non-proprietary lease. As Martin Dixon has observed ([2000] CLJ 28) 'Lord Hoffmann's explanation of why the contractual arrangement between Bruton and the trust can be regarded as a lease, even though the trust has no estate in the land, is actually an explanation of why it is a contractual licence'.

- *Uratemp Ventures Ltd v Collins* [2001]: the House of Lords held that an occupant of a room in a hotel was capable of being a tenant of a 'separate dwelling' for the purposes of the HA 1988.

LEASEHOLD COVENANTS

Leasehold covenants are promises contained in leases by which one party undertakes to do something or not do something. Some covenants are implied; others may be express:

- *The tenant's implied obligations*: keeping property in 'a tenant-like manner' (*Marden v Heyes Ltd* [1972]); to allow the landlord to enter and inspect the property (*Mint v Good* [1951]); to pay rent, rates and taxes (*United Scientific Holdings v Burnley BC* [1977]).

- The landlord's implied obligations: to permit the tenant 'quiet enjoyment' of the premises – not to harass or interfere with the tenant's enjoyment (*McCall v Abelesz* [1976]); not to derogate from grant (*Stewart v Scottish Widows & Life Assurance plc* [2005]; to ensure that dwelling houses are reasonably fit for human habitation (s 8 of the LTA 1985); to keep in repair the structure of a dwelling house let for a term of less than seven years (s 1 of the LTA 1985).

EXPRESS COVENANTS

There are many different types of covenant – two of the most common being the tenant covenanting not to assign or sublet the lease, or the landlord covenanting to repair the property.

ENFORCING COVENANTS IN LEASES CREATED BEFORE 1 JANUARY 1996

The original landlord and tenant would be in privity of contract and could therefore sue each other on the contract.

The original tenant may be liable throughout the original term of the lease, even after he has assigned the lease (*City of London Corp v Fell* [1993]). The original tenant may be able to recover from the defaulting tenant under the rule in *Moule v Garrett* [1872], or from the person to whom he directly assigned the lease under s 77 of the LPA 1925.

The original landlord may also be liable throughout the term of the lease, even after assignment of the reversion (*Stuart v Joy* [1904]).

Assignees will also generally be liable if they are in privity of estate (*Spencer's Case* [1583]) and the covenant 'touches and concerns the land' (*P & A Swift v Combined English Stores Group* [1989]).

The LPA 1925 provides that the benefit (s 141) and burden (s 142) of the landlord's covenants will pass with the reversion.

The burden of negative covenants may be enforced under the rule in *Tulk v Moxhay* [1848].

ENFORCING COVENANTS IN LEASES CREATED AFTER 31 DECEMBER 1995

- The LT(C)A 1995 applies to all landlord and tenant covenants (s 2(1)).

- The benefit and burden of all covenants, legal and equitable, will pass on assignment of the land (s 3), unless the covenants are expressed to be personal (s 3(6)).

- The benefit of a landlord's right of re-entry will also pass (s 4).

- A tenant is released from the burden and ceases to be entitled to the benefit of his covenants when he assigns the lease (s 5).

- The tenant may be required to guarantee performance of the covenants by his assignee (s 16). This is known as an authorised guarantee agreement (AGA).

- A landlord (s 6) or former landlord (s 7) may apply to be released from the benefit and burden of his covenants if he assigns the reversion. Any objection to release must be reasonable (s 8).

LANDLORD'S REMEDIES FOR BREACH OF COVENANT

- *Action for arrears of rent:* there is a six-year limitation period (s 19 of the LA 1980).

- *Damages.*

- *Injunction and specific performance*: specific performance will only be granted if it would not be oppressive to the tenant and the rules of equity have been satisfied (*Co-operative Insurance Society Ltd v Argyll Stores Ltd* [1998]). Specific performance of a repairing covenant will only be available in exceptional circumstances (*Rainbow Estates Ltd v Tokenhold* [1999]).

> ### CO-OPERATIVE INSURANCE SOCIETY LTD v ARGYLL STORES LTD [1998]
>
> **Specific performance will not be granted where performance would require constant supervision by the courts.**
>
> Facts
>
> The tenants had covenanted to keep their store open for the duration of the lease. The business deteriorated and the store was closed. The Landlord sought an order of specific performance to compel the tenant to carry on his business.
>
> Held
>
> The court refused specific performance mainly due to the difficulty of supervision.

- *Distress (or distraint)*: distress occurs when a landlord enters the demised premises and seizes the tenant's goods in satisfaction of rent arrears. A landlord should take great care before exercising this ancient remedy which, though draconian, does not infringe the European Convention on Human Rights (*Fuller v Happy Shopper Markets Ltd* [2001]).

- *Forfeiture*: if the lease contains a right of re-entry, the landlord may be able to resort to the remedy of forfeiture if the tenant breaches his covenants. The landlord may forfeit the lease either by peaceable re-entry or by bringing possession proceedings, although only the latter method is possible for residential property (s 2 of PEA 1977). If the breach of covenant is for non-payment of rent, the landlord must comply with the procedure outlined in the Common Law Procedure Act 1852. In all other circumstances he must comply with s 146 of the LPA 1925. The court has discretion to grant relief to the tenant even after the landlord has succeeded in re-entering the premises (*Billson v Residential Apartments Ltd* [1992]).

> ### BILLSON v RESIDENTIAL APARTMENTS LTD [1992]
>
> **Physical re-entry is regarded as a dubious and dangerous method of determining a lease.**
>
> Facts
> The Landlord sought to forfeit a lease against tenants who were in breach of a repairing covenant. The Landlord forcibly entered the premises early one morning, changed the locks and left a notice informing the tenants that the lease had been forfeited.
>
> Held
> The House of Lords disapproved of forcible re-entry but accepted that the Landlord was still able to use this method.

TENANT'S REMEDIES FOR BREACH OF COVENANT

- *Damages*: the tenant is entitled to be placed in the position he would have been in had there been no breach (*Calabar Properties Ltd v Stitcher* [1984]).

- *Injunction and specific performance*: specific performance of a landlord's covenant to repair is generally available to the tenant (s 17 of the LTA 1985 and *Jeune v Queens Cross Properties* [1974]).

- *Retention of rent to pay for repairs (equitable set-off)*: if the landlord takes action against the tenant for non-payment of rent and the landlord has breached his covenants to repair, the tenant may be entitled to set off the value of the repairs against his rent arrears (*Eller v Grovecrest Investments Ltd* [1995]).

METHODS OF TERMINATING LEASES

Effluxion of time
The period of the lease comes to an end. The tenant may have statutory protection, however.

Forfeiture
See above.

PROTECTION OF THE LEASE

Notice to quit

A valid notice may be served by one of a number of joint tenants (*Hammersmith & Fulham LBC v Monk* [1992] and *Notting Hill Housing Trust v Brackley* [2001]). Notices used to have to be correct in every detail in order to be effective but, since *Mannai Investment Co v Eagle Star Life Assurance Co Ltd* [1997], minor discrepancies may be disregarded if a reasonable recipient would have realised the intended effect of the notice. The decision in *Mannai* appears to have caused a great deal of uncertainty (see *Diamond and Sandham* [2004] *Conv* 361).

Surrender

The tenant surrenders his lease to the landlord who accepts the surrender.

Merger

The tenant acquires the landlord's reversion, thereby merging it with the lease.

Disclaimer

The tenant denies his landlord's title.

Enlargement

When a tenant holds a lease which was originally granted for 300 years or more and there are still 200 years or more left to run, he may enlarge his interest to a freehold (s 153 of the LPA 1925).

Frustration

Frustration will rarely apply to a lease. However, it may be possible if the lease becomes incapable of performance for a significant proportion of the term (*National Carriers Ltd v Panalpina Ltd* [1981]).

You should now be confident that you would be able to tick all the boxes on the checklist at the beginning of this chapter. To check your knowledge of Leases why not visit the companion website and take the Multiple Choice Question test. Check your understanding of the terms and vocabulary used in this chapter with the flashcard glossary.

8 Mortgages

- Creation of legal mortgages
- Creation of equitable mortgages
- Equity of redemption
- Undue influence and misrepresentation
- Remedies of the mortgagee
- Protection of mortgages

> A mortgage is a transaction under which land or chattels are given as security for the payment of a debt or the discharge of some other obligation.
>
> (*Santley v Wilde* [1899])

The owner of the land (the mortgagor) receives a loan in return for which he grants a mortgage to the mortgagee (nowadays usually a bank or building society). The agreement continues until the loan is repaid and the mortgage is redeemed.

CREATION OF LEGAL MORTGAGES

FREEHOLD LAND

Two methods (s 85(1) of the LPA 1925):

- By demise.
- By legal charge.

Legal mortgages of registered land cannot be created by demise since 13 October 2003 (s 23(1) of the LRA 2002).

Freehold land by demise

Mortgagor grants a lease to the mortgagee subject to a provision for cesser on redemption. A first or only mortgagee takes a term for 3,000 years (s 85(2) of the LPA 1925). Note: can now only be created if the land is unregistered.

Freehold land by legal charge

The mortgagee has the same protection, powers and remedies as if a mortgage of 3,000 years had been granted in his favour (s 87(1) of the LPA 1925).

LEASEHOLD LAND

Two methods (s 86(1) of the LPA 1925):

- By sub-demise.
- By legal charge.

Legal mortgages of registered land cannot be created by sub-demise since 13 October 2003 (s 23(1) of the LRA 2002).

Leasehold land by sub-demise

Mortgagor grants a sublease to the mortgagee subject to a provision for cesser on redemption. A first or only mortgagee takes a term ten days less than that of the mortgagor (s 86(2) of the LPA 1925).

Note: can now only be created if the land is unregistered.

The mortgagee has the same protection, powers and remedies as if a sub-term less by one day than the term vested in the mortgagor had been granted in his favour (s 87(1) of the LPA 1925).

CREATION OF EQUITABLE MORTGAGES

- By valid contract under the rule in *Walsh v Lonsdale* [1882]. The contract must be capable of specific performance and must comply with the relevant formalities (s 2 of the LP(MP)A 1989).

- By an express equitable charge.

A mortgage of an equitable interest under a trust is always equitable. It must be in writing and signed by the mortgagor (s 53(1)(c) of the LPA 1925).

The method of creating a mortgage by deposit of title deeds or Land Certificate has not been possible since s 2 of the LP(MP)A 1989 came into force (*United Bank of Kuwait v Sahib* [1997]). After 26 September 1989, any attempt to create a mortgage by deposit alone will be ineffective and may lead to a successful negligence claim by the purported mortgagee (see *Dean v Allin & Watts* [2001] – solicitors liable after mortgage by deposit of title deeds was deemed void).

THE MORTGAGOR'S EQUITY OF REDEMPTION

When the mortgagor grants a mortgage, he grants the mortgagee an interest in his land which is the equivalent of a legal estate (a term of years). The mortgagee therefore has a right to possession of the mortgaged property. The mortgagor is left with few legal rights to his property; but he does have his equity of redemption.

The equity of redemption is a collection of rights which may be summed up by the maxim 'once a mortgage always a mortgage' (*Seton v Slade* [1802]):

the mortgagor must be free to redeem the mortgage at any time after the date set for redemption has passed (the date set for redemption is typically about six months after the creation of the mortgage). The equity of redemption comprises a number of rights, the most notable being the following:

- *'There should be no clogs or fetters on the equity of redemption'*: the mortgagee must not attempt to exclude the right to redeem. Equity will not permit an option to purchase the mortgaged property in the mortgage deed, even if the option constitutes 'a perfectly fair bargain' (*Samuel v Jarrah Timber and Wood Paving Corp Ltd* [1904]). An option to purchase the mortgaged property may be valid if granted after the mortgage, however, because there is little likelihood of unconscionable conduct (*Reeve v Lisle* [1902]).

▶ FAIRCLOUGH v SWAN BREWERY CO LTD [1912]

A clause in a mortgage that deters the mortgagor's right to redeem will usually be invalid.

Facts

A term in the mortgage agreement on a long lease of a public house was challenged as it postponed the right to redemption until six weeks before the end of the lease.

Held

The clause was held to be void.

- *'There should be no unreasonable postponement of the right to redeem'*: equity will prevent the mortgagee from gaining an unfair advantage (*Fairclough v Swan Brewery Co Ltd* [1912]). However, if the parties are two competent parties, acting under expert advice, and dealing at arm's length, the agreement will stand (*Knightsbridge Estates Trust Ltd v Byrne* [1940] – redemption not possible for 40 years).

▶ KNIGHTSBRIDGE ESTATES TRUST LTD v BYRNE [1940]

A term postponing redemption may be upheld where the arrangement is of a commercial nature.

CREATION OF LEGAL MORTGAGES

> Facts
>
> A company mortgaged its freehold property on terms that the mortgage would be paid back over 40 years. Later the mortgagor wished to redeem early but the mortgagee objected.
>
> Held
>
> The redemption clause was valid as the arrangement was of a commercial nature made between two businessmen who clearly understood the nature of the transaction.

- '*There should be no unfair collateral advantages*': a collateral advantage is an agreement contained in a mortgage or a lease which does not relate to the mortgage or lease. The collateral advantage often takes the form of a solus agreement, whereby a mortgagor or lessee covenants only to purchase supplies from the mortgagee or lessor. Such an agreement will usually be enforceable only for the duration of the mortgage (*Biggs v Hoddinott* [1898]) 'and necessarily comes to an end upon payment off of the loan' (*Noakes and Co Ltd v Rice* [1902]). If the mortgagor is able to prove that the collateral advantage is fair and that it is not a clog on the equity of redemption, it may be enforceable after the mortgage has been redeemed (*Kreglinger v New Patagonia Meat and Cold Storage Co* [1914]). Solus agreements may also be in restraint of trade and therefore contrary to Art 81 of the EEC Treaty.

- '*There should be no oppressive or unconscionable terms*': the court may reduce a rate of interest which is deemed to be unconscionable (*Cityland and Property (Holdings) Ltd v Dabrah* [1968] – an annual rate of 19 per cent reduced to 7 per cent). However, the test is unconscionability and harsh terms will be allowed when businessmen are dealing 'at arm's length' (*Multiservice Bookbinding Ltd v Marden* [1979]). If provided for in the agreement, the mortgagee may alter interest rates, provided that he does so in good faith, for valid commercial reasons, and not for dishonest or improper purposes (*Paragon Finance plc v Nash* [2001]). Many first mortgages of residential property will be regulated by the code of practice contained within the Financial Service and Markets Act 2000, which protects against extortionate credit bargains. Second mortgages may fall under the protection of ss 19–22 of the Consumer Credit Act 2006 which allows the court to intervene where a relationship under a credit agreement is unfair to the debtor.

> ### KREGLINGER v NEW PATAGONIA MEAT AND COLD STORAGE CO [1914]

Collateral advantages in commercial agreements that are not unconscionable will be valid for the term of a mortgage.

Facts

A meat company mortgaged its property to a wool broker. The mortgage contained a term that the mortgagor would offer its sheepskins to the mortgagees to purchase for a period of five years. The mortgage was redeemed after two years and the mortgagor challenged his liability under the option.

Held

The term was held to be reasonable and could be regarded as a separate agreement to the mortgage arrangement.

UNDUE INFLUENCE AND MISREPRESENTATION

Mortgagees themselves rarely exert undue influence or misrepresent the terms of the mortgage. However, the mortgagee may be unable to enforce the mortgage if it has either actual or constructive notice of undue influence exerted by a third party, or if the third party is deemed to have been acting as the agent of the mortgagee (*Kings North Trust Ltd v Bell* [1986]).

UNDUE INFLUENCE EXERTED BY A THIRD PARTY

IS THE MORTGAGEE TAINTED WITH UNDUE INFLUENCE EXERTED BY A THIRD PARTY?

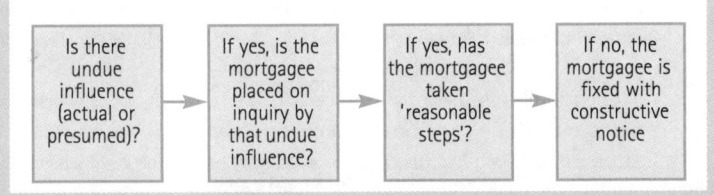

Is there undue influence (actual or presumed)? → If yes, is the mortgagee placed on inquiry by that undue influence? → If yes, has the mortgagee taken 'reasonable steps'? → If no, the mortgagee is fixed with constructive notice

CREATION OF LEGAL MORTGAGES

Actual and presumed undue influence: if the claimant is able to establish actual undue influence he does not have to prove that the transaction has been disadvantageous to him (*CIBC Mortgages plc v Pitt* [1994]). Undue influence may be presumed in two circumstances: when the relationship between the parties automatically gives rise to the presumption (solicitor/client; doctor/patient, etc – identified as type 2(A) in *Barclays Bank plc v O'Brien* [1994]); or when the *de facto* relationship between the parties was one of trust and confidence (husband/wife or parent/child may fall into this category – type 2(B)). In cases of presumed undue influence, the claimant must establish that the transaction was to his disadvantage (*Dunbar Bank plc v Nadeem* [1998]).

Placing the mortgagee on inquiry: the mortgagee will be on inquiry if the nature of the transaction is such that there is a substantial risk of undue influence (*Barclays Bank plc v O'Brien* [1994] – a wife mortgaged her share in the matrimonial home to act as surety for her husband's business debts; she obtained no advantage from the transaction).

The leading case in this area is *Royal Bank of Scotland v Etridge (No 2)* [2001]. Since this case, a lender will be put on inquiry in *all* cases where a relationship is non-commercial.

Taking reasonable steps: the steps were enunciated by Lord Nicholls in *Royal Bank of Scotland plc v Etridge (No 2)* [2001]:

- the bank must take reasonable steps to satisfy itself that the wife has understood the ramifications of the proposed transaction;

- if the bank is not to provide face-to-face advice itself, the wife should be asked to choose a solicitor to advise her;

- the bank must provide the solicitor with details of the husband's financial circumstances;

- the bank may rely on the advice given by the solicitor unless it is aware of adverse circumstances that were not made known to the solicitor;

- the solicitor must hold a face-to-face meeting without the husband;

- he must explain to the wife: the effect of the transaction; the nature of the risk, considering the husband's financial circumstances; he must emphasise that the decision rests with the wife; and he must confirm that she wishes to proceed with the transaction.

The remedy: if the bank is fixed with constructive notice of the undue influence or misrepresentation, the charge will be set aside in its entirety (*TSB Bank v Camfield* [1995]).

▶ BARCLAYS BANK PLC v O'BRIEN [1994]

A lender will be put on notice when a transaction is not to the financial benefit of a wife and she has been induced to sign documents as a result of misrepresentation or undue influence.

Facts

The wife signed a mortgage deed for what her husband had represented to be a short term loan for £60,000. In reality the mortgage was to cover all of his business debts. She took no independent advice. The husband defaulted on the mortgage and the wife argued that the debt should be set aside for undue influence.

Held

The bank was deemed to have constructive notice of the husband's misrepresentation, and the mortgage was held to be void against the wife.

THE REMEDIES OF THE MORTGAGEE

The right to sue on the covenant to repay

Section 20(1) of the LA 1980 sets a 12-year limitation period for recovery of the principal sum. The limitation period for the recovery of interest is six years (s 20(5)).

The power of sale

Available when the mortgage has been granted by deed – equitable mortgagees may apply under s 91(2) of the LPA 1925).

The power must have arisen (s 101 of the LPA 1925) and have become exercisable (s 103).

CREATION OF LEGAL MORTGAGES

According to s 103 of the LPA 1925, the power of sale arises when: either the mortgagor has been in default for three months following the service upon him of a notice requiring payment of the mortgage money; or some interest on the mortgage has remained unpaid for two months after becoming due; or there has been a breach of some mortgage term other than a covenant to repay.

When the property is sold the mortgagee holds the proceeds in trust (s 105).

After costs have been met and mortgagees repaid in order of priority, any surplus is to be paid to the mortgagor (*Halifax Building Society v Thomas* [1996]).

The mortgagee has a duty to obtain a true market value for the property, but not necessarily the best price possible (*Cuckmere Brick Co Ltd v Mutual Finance* [1971]).

The right to possession
Available to legal mortgagees.

The right to possession does not depend on the mortgagor's default – the mortgagor may go into possession 'before the ink is dry on the mortgage' (*Four-Maids Ltd v Dudley Marshall Ltd* [1957]).

The court may grant relief to a mortgagor of a dwelling house if he is likely to be able to repay sums due under the mortgage within a reasonable period (s 36 of the AJA 1970).

If the mortgagor intends to repay the mortgage by instalments, the starting point for determining a reasonable period is the remaining term of the mortgage (*Cheltenham and Gloucester BS v Norgan* [1996]), but a much shorter period of relief will be granted if the mortgagor intends to repay the mortgage by selling the property (*Target Home Loans Ltd v Clothier* [1994]).

The time for determining whether or not a property is a dwelling is the time when proceedings are initiated (*Royal Bank of Scotland v Miller* [2001]).

If the mortgagee sells the property without bringing an action or takes peaceable possession of the property whilst the mortgagor is not present at the property, the mortgagor may not claim relief under s 36 (*Ropaigealach v Barclays Bank plc* [1999]). The courts have rejected the claim that the viability of the mortgagor to claim relief in such circumstances is in breach of ECHR rights (*Horsham Properties Group Ltd v Clark* [2008]).

> ### ROYAL BANK OF SCOTLAND PLC v ETRIDGE (No 2) [2001]
>
> **A mortgagee must take reasonable steps to ensure that a mortgagor is not acting under the undue influence of another party.**
>
> Facts
>
> The case concerned eight conjoined appeals. In all cases, the mortgages were for the benefit of the husband and the issue was whether the mortgage could be set aside for undue influence.
>
> Held
>
> Specific guidelines were laid down on the steps that a lender should take to avoid being affected by the undue influence of the borrower. The lender must obtain confirmation and a certificate from the advising solicitor confirming that he has given independent advice to the wife.

The right to appoint a receiver

Available to a legal mortgagee (s 101(1) of the LPA 1925) – equitable mortgagees may apply under s 37(1) of the Supreme Court Act 1981).

A receiver may be appointed if the power of sale has become exercisable (s 109 of the LPA 1925).

A receiver owes a duty to the mortgagor to manage the property with due diligence (*Medforth v Blake* [1999]).

The right to foreclose

When a mortgagee obtains an order for foreclosure the mortgagor's equity of redemption is extinguished and the property is in effect transferred to the mortgagee (ss 88 and 89 of the LPA 1925).

Because it is such a draconian remedy, foreclosure is rarely granted, the court usually preferring to exercise its discretion under s 91(2) to award sale in lieu of foreclosure. If the court decides to allow foreclosure, an order nisi will be granted, followed by an order absolute.

PROTECTION OF MORTGAGES

- A legal mortgage of unregistered land, which is protected by deposit of title deeds, is binding the world and does not require further protection. If it is not protected by deposit of title deeds it should be registered as a Class C(i) land charge in the Land Charges Register.

- An equitable mortgage of unregistered land should be protected by entry of either a Class C(iii) or a Class C(iv) land charge.

- A legal mortgage of registered land should be entered as a legal charge against the title to be charged.

- An equitable mortgage of registered land should be entered as a minor interest against the title to be charged.

You should now be confident that you would be able to tick all the boxes on the checklist at the beginning of this chapter. To check your knowledge of Mortgages why not visit the companion website and take the Multiple Choice Question test. Check your understanding of the terms and vocabulary used in this chapter with the flashcard glossary.

9

Easements and *profits à prendre*

- Definition of an easement
- Characteristics of an easement
- Examples of common easements
- Creating an easement by grant
- Implied grant of necessity
- The rule in *Wheeldon v Burrows* [1879]
- Law of Property Act 1925, section 62
- Prescription
- Reservation of easements
- Protection of easements
- Alteration and extinguishment of easements

EASEMENTS AND *PROFITS À PRENDRE*

An easement is a right exercised over one plot of land (the servient tenement) for the benefit of another plot of land (the dominant tenement). We usually imagine an easement as a right of way or right to light, but there are many other rights that may be classified as easements, for example, a right to use a lavatory (*Miller v Emcer Products* [1956]) or a right to use neighbouring land as an airfield (*Dowty Boulton Paul Ltd v Wolverhampton Corp (No 2)* [1976]).

An easement must be distinguished from other similar rights:

- *Easements*: rights exercised for the benefit of one plot of land over another.

- *Profits à prendre*: rights to take something from land (eg, wood – a profit of estovers).

The law regarding profits is similar to the law of easements.

- *Licences*: permissions to do something on the land. Licences are merely personal rights and are not interests in the land.

- *Customary rights*: rights in favour of the inhabitants of a particular community (*Mercer v Denne* [1905] – rights of members of a locality to dry fishing nets on the foreshore). Customary rights must be ancient, reasonable, certain and continuous (*Lockwood v Wood* [1844]). They are overriding interests for the purposes of registered land (para 4 of Sched 3 to the LRA 2002).

- *Public rights*: rights which are exercisable by any member of the public, such as public rights of way. Like easements, they may be acquired by prescription (long user), but they are not appurtenant to land. Public rights are overriding interests in registered land (para 5 of Sched 3 to the LRA 2002).

- *Natural rights*: natural rights are usually protected by the law of torts. They include a right of support for land (*Leakey v National Trust* [1980]; *Holbeck Hall Hotel Ltd v Scarborough BC* [2000]).

IS THE RIGHT CLAIMED CAPABLE OF BEING AN EASEMENT?
The answer to this question is found in the four defining characteristics of an easement, as listed by Dankwerts J in *Re Ellenborough Park* [1956].

RE ELLENBOROUGH PARK [1956]

The leading case in establishing the four characteristics of an easement.

Facts

The owners of land adjacent to a park claimed that the right to enjoy the use of the park could be recognised as an easement.

Held

The characteristics of an easement were stated and the right was found to meet the criteria.

1 There must be dominant and servient tenement

An easement can only exist appurtenant to land. There must be two plots of land: one to take the benefit of the easement and another to take the burden. A profit, on the other hand, may exist 'in gross' – without a dominant tenement (*Bettison v Langton* [2002]).

2 The right claimed must accommodate the dominant tenement

The right must be of benefit to the dominant land and not just to a particular owner of it (*Hill v Tupper* [1863]). The two plots of land do not have to be contiguous (*Re Ellenborough Park* [1956]), but they must be close enough for the dominant tenement to obtain some benefit (*Bailey v Stephens* [1862]). The right must not be purely recreational (*Mouncey v Ismay* [1865]), but it is possible to acquire an easement to use a garden (*Re Ellenborough Park* [1956]; *Mulvaney v Gough* [2002]).

3 The dominant and servient tenements must be owned by different persons

Obviously, you cannot have an easement over your own land (*Roe v Siddons* [1888]). However, if a landowner owns two plots of land and he exercises rights over one plot for the benefit of the other, such rights (known as quasi-easements) may become proper easements if one plot of land is sold (see *Wheeldon v Burrows* [1879] below). A tenant may acquire an easement over the land of his landlord.

4 The right claimed must be capable of forming the subject matter of a grant

There must be a capable grantor and a capable grantee.

The right must be sufficiently definite. There is no right to a view (*Aldred's Case* [1610]), or a right to light other than through a defined aperture.

The right must be in the nature of rights traditionally categorised as easements, but 'the categories . . . must alter and expand with the changes that take place in the circumstances of mankind' (*Dyce v Lady James Hay* [1852]).

The right must not amount to exclusive or joint user (*Copeland v Greenhalf* [1952]; *Grigsby v Melville* [1974]).

The right must not involve the servient owner in expenditure. An exception is easements of fencing (*Crow v Wood* [1971]).

> ### ▶ COPELAND v GREENHALF [1952]
>
> **An easement cannot exist where there is exclusive use or joint user.**
>
> Facts
> A wheelwright claimed an easement to store and repair vehicles on neighbouring land.
>
> Held
> The court held that the right could not form an easement as the claim amounted to exclusive use of part of the servient land.

THE EXTENT OF SOME COMMON EASEMENTS

Rights of way

- The maintenance of the right of way is the responsibility of the grantee, unless there are circumstances to indicate the contrary (*Miller v Hancock* [1893]).

- The grantee may repair and improve the way if it was within the contemplation of the parties at the time of the grant (*Gerrard v Cooke* [1806]).

If the right was acquired by prescription, the grantee may repair, but not improve, the way (*Mills v Silver* [1991]).

- Increased usage will only be permitted if it was within the contemplation of the parties at the time of the grant (*Jelbert v Davis* [1968]). If the right was acquired by prescription, increased usage will be permitted provided that the nature of the user does not change (*British Railways Board v Glass* [1965]; *Loder v Gaden* [1999]).

- A right of way acquired for the benefit of one plot of land may not be used to gain access to land adjoining the dominant tenement (*Harris v Flower* [1904]; *Peacock v Custins* [2002]; *Das v Linden Mews Ltd* [2002]).

Easements of light

The right claimed must be a right to light through a defined aperture (eg, a window).

In order to be actionable, interference with the right must affect the claimant's use and enjoyment of his land (*Colls v Home and Colonial Stores Ltd* [1904]).

Even if the claimant succeeds in demonstrating that use of his building has been (or would be) affected, if the court decides that granting an injunction would be oppressive he may not be entitled to an injunction; he might have to rely upon damages in lieu (see *Midtown Ltd v City of London Real Property Co Ltd* [2005]).

Even a right to a high intensity of light may be acquired as an easement (*Allen v Greenwood* [1980] – right of light to a greenhouse).

Easements of car parking

It is possible to acquire an easement to park a car, but not in a specific space. The right must not leave the servient owner without any reasonable use of any part of his land (*London & Blenheim Estates Ltd v Ladbroke Retail Parks Ltd* [1994]; *Batchelor v Marlow* [2001]). In *Moncrieff v Jamieson* [2007] the court confirmed that 'sole use' of an easement would be possible provided that the servient owner retained 'possession and control' of the land – see also *Virdi v Chana* [2008].

> ### LONDON & BLENHEIM ESTATES LTD v LADBROKE RETAIL PARKS LTD [1994]

A right to park is capable of existing as an easement provided it does not leave the servient owner without any reasonable use of his land.

Facts

The owner of a shopping centre claimed a right of easement for his customers to park on a central car park.

Held

The right was found to constitute an easement because it did not deprive the servient owner of the right to use his land.

> ### BATCHELOR v MARLOW [2001]

Where a right would leave the servient owner without any reasonable use of his land an easement will be rejected.

Facts

The claimant sought the right to park six cars on a verge of land on Monday and Friday each week between the hours of 8.30 am – 6.30 pm. Such use would prevent the owner from using the land during these periods of time.

Held

The claim was rejected as use would leave the servient owner with only minimal use of his land.

CREATING AN EASEMENT

The requirements of *Re Ellenborough Park* [1956] merely help us to decide whether a right is capable of being an easement. In order for the right to be enforceable, it must have been validly created and, if the right is to bind third parties, it may need to be protected. Easements may be acquired by grant or by reservation.

METHODS OF CREATING EASEMENTS BY GRANT

Express grant
Formal grants must be by deed and they are usually incorporated into a conveyance or transfer of the legal estate. They must be 'for an interest equivalent to an estate in fee simple absolute in possession or a term of years absolute' to be legal (s 1(2)(a) of the LPA 1925). Post LRA 2002, the easement must be registered to be legal.

Informal grant
Easements may be created by valid contract under the rule in *Walsh v Lonsdale* [1882]. The grant relies on the remedy of specific performance and will be equitable only.

Estoppel
An easement may be acquired by estoppel (*ER Ives Ltd v High* [1967]).

Statute
Many easements were created long ago by the Inclosure Acts. More recently, easements have been created by statute in favour of public utilities (eg. for gas or electricity pylons, for cables or pipes, etc.). Such easements are often termed wayleaves.

A statutory licence may be obtained by a landowner if he needs to enter onto neighbouring land in order to perform work which is reasonably necessary for the preservation of his land (Access to Neighbouring Land Act 1992). The order awarded by the court under this Act is similar to an easement, but the right of access terminates when the work has been completed.

Implied grant of necessity
A grant will only be implied out of necessity if it is impossible to enjoy land without such a grant (*Wong v Beaumont Property Trust Ltd* [1965]). The obvious example is when a plot of land would be landlocked without the implication of an easement.

Grant implied to give effect to the common intention of the parties
Nickerson v Barraclough [1981].

The rule in *Wheeldon v Burrows* [1879]
The rule implies an easement when a number of requirements are satisfied:

There must be unity of seisin before the grant: when a landowner owns two adjacent plots of land and he exercises a quasi-easement over one plot for the benefit of another, the quasi-easement may become a proper easement if he sells the dominant land. Provided that:

- the right is continuous and apparent at the time of the grant; and

- the right is necessary for the reasonable enjoyment of the land (*Wheeler v JJ Saunders Ltd* [1995]).

> **WHEELER v JJ SAUNDERS LTD [1995]**
>
> A claim to an easement under the rule in *Wheeldon v Burrows* will only succeed if the dominant land cannot be enjoyed without the right.
>
> Facts
> A claimant purchased land which had access over the defendant's land. When the defendant built a wall blocking off the access, the claimant argued that the access constituted an easement under the rule in *Wheeldon v Burrows*.
>
> Held
> The access was not necessary for the reasonable enjoyment of the land as there was an alternative access which did not involve the defendant's land.

Section 62 of the Law of Property Act 1925
Section 62 has been interpreted as being capable of turning a licence into an easement. As there has to be diversity of ownership before the grant, s 62 usually applies when a landlord renews a lease (*Wright v Macadam* [1949]) or when he sells the freehold to his tenant (*Hair v Gillman* [2000]). In order to avoid the consequences of s 62, a landlord may either revoke the licence before the conveyance or state a contrary intention in the conveyance (s 62(4)). There are two requirements:

- s 62 requires a conveyance;

- there must be diversity of ownership before the grant (*Sovmots Investments Ltd v S of S for the Environment* [1979] the opposite of *Wheeldon v Burrows*).

- the diversity of ownership requirement was considered to be unnecessary when the right claimed is continuous and apparent in *P & S Platt v Crouch* [2005].

Prescription (rights acquired by long user)
There are three different methods of acquiring easements by prescription:

- *Common law prescription*: the claimant has to establish use since 1189.

- *Lost modern grant*: if the claimant can prove 20 years' use, the law may presume a lost grant (*Dalton v Angus and Co* [1881]).

- *The Prescription Act 1832*: after 20 years, a claim to an easement cannot be defeated by evidence that it began after 1189; after 40 years the right becomes indefeasible unless the original use was as a result of consent or agreement (s 2); the periods for profits are 30 and 60 years (s 1); rights to light become indefeasible after 20 years (s 3). All periods must be 'next before some suit or action' (s 4).

Whatever method is relied upon, there are a number of requirements:

- The user must be the fee simple owner (*Simmonds v Dobson* [1991]).

- The user must be continuous (the right must not have been abandoned).

- The user must be as of right (*R v Oxfordshire CC ex parte Sunningwell Parish Council* [2000]), which means user *nec vi* (without force), *nec clam* (without secrecy), and *nec precario* (it must not be exercised as a result of permission given by the servient owner).

RESERVATION OF EASEMENTS

Express reservation
In the event of doubt or ambivalence the terms will be construed against the party reserving the right.

Implied reservation of necessity

A reservation will only be implied if the land is landlocked or is incapable of use without the reservation (*Union Lighterage Co v London Graving Dock Co* [1902]). As a result, implied reservation is very rare – for a rare example, see *Sweet v Sommer* [2004].

Reservation implied to give effect to the common intention of the parties

A reservation will rarely be implied to give effect to the intention of the parties (*Re Webb's Lease* [1951]; *Holaw (470) v Stockton Estates Ltd* [2000]). A notable exception is *Peckham v Ellison* [1998].

PROTECTION OF EASEMENTS

Unregistered land

Legal easements and profits are rights *in rem* and bind the whole world.

Equitable easements created after 1925 are registrable as Class D(iii) land charges; if created before 1926 they are subject to the doctrine of notice.

Registered land

Most legal easements will be entered on the register against the title affected. Those legal easements which are not on the register may override first registration (para 3 of Sched 1 to the LRA 2002). In order to override a registered disposition under para 3 of Sched 3, the easement must have been exercised within the past year or it must be within the actual knowledge of the purchaser, or the easement must have been discoverable by a reasonably careful inspection of the land.

Equitable easements should be entered as minor interests.

ALTERATION AND EXTINGUISHMENT OF EASEMENTS

Alteration or realignment of an easement is rarely possible without the agreement of both parties (*B & Q plc v Liverpool and Lancashire Properties Ltd* [2001]), but in *Greenwich Health Care NHS Trust v London & Quadrant Housing Trust* [1998] realignment of a right of way was permitted because realignment was of considerable public benefit.

Easements do not lapse, but there are a number of ways by which they may come to an end:

- *Express release*: the dominant owner releases the servient owner from the obligation by deed.

- *Unity of possession and ownership*: you cannot have an easement over your own land.

- *Implied release*: there must be an intention on the part of the dominant owner to abandon the easement permanently. This may be difficult to prove – in *Benn v Hardinge* [1992], a nonuser for 175 years was not sufficient for the implication of abandonment without evidence of an intention to abandon permanently (*Gotobed v Pridmore* [1970]; *CDC2020 v Ferreira* [2005]). The Law Commission (Report 254) recommended that there should be a rebuttable presumption of abandonment if the right has not been used for 20 years.

You should now be confident that you would be able to tick all the boxes on the checklist at the beginning of this chapter. To check your knowledge of Easements and *profits à prendre* why not visit the companion website and take the Multiple Choice Question test. Check your understanding of the terms and vocabulary used in this chapter with the flashcard glossary.

Freehold covenants

Definition of a freehold covenant

Original parties

Running the benefit of covenants at law

Running the benefit of a covenant in equity

Running the burden of a covenant at law

Running the burden of a covenant in equity

Positive covenants

Discharge and modification of covenants

Remedies for breach of covenant

FREEHOLD COVENANTS

DEFINITIONS OF A FREEHOLD COVENANT

This chapter is concerned with freehold covenants, that is, covenants affecting freehold land. A covenant is merely a promise or a contract. The word 'covenant' used to be used as a synonym for the word 'contract', but it is now usually used in a more technical sense to mean a 'promise', made by deed, to use land (or not to use land) in a certain way or for a certain purpose. Consider the following example:

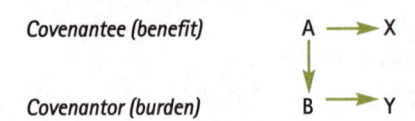

Covenantee (benefit)   A ⟶ X

Covenantor (burden)   B ⟶ Y

In the example, B has entered into a covenant with A. Let us imagine that the covenant is a promise that B will not use his property for business purposes. The person who makes the promise, in this case B, is known as the covenantor, and the person to whom the promise is made, in this case A, is the covenantee. Because A and B are in privity of contract, A is able to enforce the promise against B.

In time, however, the land will be sold. If A sells his land to X, who was not a party to the original contract, X will want to enforce the covenant against B. In order to do so, X must establish that he has the benefit of the covenant. In order to do this, the benefit of the covenant must pass with the land (the term that we usually use is that the covenant must 'run with the land'). X is known as the assignee of the covenantee.

If B sells his land to Y (the assignee of the covenantor), it must be established that the burden of the covenant has run with the land to Y before he can be sued on the covenant. If both plots of land have been sold, X may want to sue Y, in which case both the benefit and the burden of the covenant must have run with the land. The rules for running covenants at law differ from the rules in equity.

THE ORIGINAL PARTIES

In the above example, A is able to enforce the covenant against B because they are in privity of contract. However, if B covenanted for the benefit of A, his successors in title and 'the owners and occupiers of adjoining property', the owners of adjoining land, may take the benefit of the covenant because the covenant has been made for their benefit (s 56 of the LPA 1925; *White v Bijou Mansions* [1938]; *Re Shaw's Application* [1995]. (NB: s 56 requires that the covenant must be expressed to be made **with** third parties, not simply expressed for their benefit.)

CONTRACTS (RIGHTS OF THIRD PARTIES) ACT 1999

C(ROTP)A 1999 provides that a person may enforce a contract 'in his own right' if the contract either provides that he may or if it 'purports to confer a benefit upon him'.

C(ROTP)A applies only to contracts created after 11 May 2000.

It provides that rights may be enforced by the third party provided that he is expressly identified in the contract by name or 'a member of a class or as answering a particular description'.

For the purposes of C(ROTP)A, persons described generically need not be in existence when the contract is entered into.

There is no requirement that the covenant should 'touch and concern' the land, nor even that the third party seeking to enforce the covenant should be entitled to an estate in the land.

RUNNING THE BENEFIT OF COVENANTS AT LAW

There are four requirements:

- The covenant must 'touch and concern' the land. It must not be purely personal.

- The parties must have intended the benefit to run with the land. This will generally be presumed by virtue of s 78 of the LPA 1925.

- The covenantee must hold a legal estate in the land. The covenantor does not have to own any land (*The Prior's Case* [1368]).

- The assignee of the covenantee must also hold a legal estate in the land. It does not have to be the same legal estate (*Smith and Snipes Hall Farm v River Douglas Catchment Board* [1949]).

> SMITH AND SNIPES HALL FARM v RIVER DOUGLAS CATCHMENT BOARD [1949]

A covenant can be enforced by a successor in title to the original covenantee if it touches and concerns the covenantee's land.

Facts
RDCB covenanted with Mrs Smith that they would improve and undertake the necessary repairs to the river banks to prevent her land from flooding. Mrs Smith sold her land to SHF. Later SHF attempted to enforce the covenant against RDCB.

Held
The covenant was held to touch and concern the land and as such the benefit had been successfully passed to SHF and they were able to enforce it.

RUNNING THE BENEFIT OF COVENANTS IN EQUITY
There are three methods:

By assignment
The benefit of the covenant may be expressly assigned by the covenantee to his successor. There are three requirements (*Miles v Easter* [1933]): the covenant must have been taken for the protection or benefit of land owned by the covenantee at the date of the covenant; the assignment must be contemporaneous with the transfer of the dominant land; and the dominant tenement must be ascertainable.

By annexation
The annexation may be expressed or implied by virtue of s 78 of the LPA 1925 (*Federated Homes Ltd v Mill Lodge Properties Ltd* [1980]), unless the parties have expressed a contrary intention (*Roake v Chadha* [1984]).

The benefited land must be clearly identified (*Renals v Cowlishaw* [1978]; *Crest Nicholson Residential Ltd v McAllister* [2004]).

FREEHOLD COVENANTS

> ### FEDERATED HOMES LTD v MILL LODGE PROPERTIES LTD [1980]
>
> By virtue of s 78 LPA 1925 a covenant relating to land must be construed as if it has been made with the covenantee and his successors if it touches and concerns the land.
>
> Facts
>
> The defendants purchased a plot and entered into a covenant not to build more than 300 houses on it. The claimants later purchased two plots of land, but the benefit of the covenant was expressly assigned to the first plot only. When the defendants tried to exceed their building limit, the claimants sought to enforce the covenant for the benefit of the second plot of land.
>
> Held
>
> The covenant could be enforced. It had been statutorily annexed to the land by operation of s 78.

By scheme of development (building scheme)

Schemes of development are usually created by a developer who obtains identical covenants from each purchaser of properties on the development. The covenants may then be enforced by any member of the development against any member who breaches the covenants. The original requirements were laid down in *Elliston v Reacher* [1908]:

> Plaintiff and defendant must acquire title from a common vendor.
>
> The vendor must have laid out the scheme in lots.
>
> The covenants must have been intended to benefit all of the lots.
>
> Both purchaser and defendant must have purchased their properties with knowledge of the scheme and with an intention to be bound.
>
> The area affected by the scheme must be clearly defined (added by *Reid v Bickerstaff* [1909]).

FREEHOLD COVENANTS

> ### ▶ ELLISTON v REACHER [1908]
>
> Covenants can be passed in equity under a building scheme if certain requirements are met.
>
> Facts
>
> A developer sold a number of plots to different individuals imposing identical covenants in all of the conveyances. Later the court had to decide whether these covenants could be enforced against the original covenantor.
>
> Held
>
> The covenants could be enforced provided that there was a common vendor and the vendor had laid out the scheme in lots which could all benefit from the covenants.

The absence of the third requirement did not prevent the finding of a building scheme in *Baxter v Four Oaks Properties* [1965], and the absence of the first requirement was not fatal in *Re Dolphin's Conveyance* [1970]. The more modern cases have tended to concentrate on the requirements 'reciprocity of obligation' and an intention to establish a system of 'local laws' (*Jamaica Life Assurance Society v Hillsborough Ltd* [1989]); see also: *Oliver v Saunders Developments Ltd* [2006].

A landlord may also create a letting scheme whereby tenants may enforce obligations between themselves (*Williams v Kiley* [2002]).

RUNNING THE BURDEN AT LAW

The burden cannot run at common law because an obligation cannot be enforced against anybody who is not a party to the covenant (*Austerberry v Corp of Oldham* [1885]).

> ### ▶ AUSTERBERRY v CORPORATION OF OLDHAM [1885]
>
> The burden of a covenant cannot be enforced at common law against a successor in title of the original covenantor.

FREEHOLD COVENANTS

> Facts
>
> The original covenantor had covenanted to construct a new road and keep it in good repair. The Corporation of Oldham later acquired the land and tried to enforce repair costs in accordance with the covenant.
>
> Held
>
> The court determined that the burden of a covenant cannot run at common law.

RUNNING THE BURDEN IN EQUITY

The burden of a covenant may run in equity under the rule in *Tulk v Moxhay* [1848]. In *Tulk*, it was decided that a purchaser of land from the covenantor is bound by the covenant if he purchased the land with notice of the covenant. For covenants created before 1926, the rule as to notice remains the same, but covenants created after 1925 must be registered in order to bind the assignee of the covenantor. If title to the land is registered, the covenant should be entered as a notice at the Land Registry; if the land is unregistered it should be entered as a Class D(ii) land charge in the Land Charges Register.

There are also four further conditions precedent before the burden will run (*Haywood v Brunswick Permanent Benefit Building Society* [1881]) under the rule in *Tulk v Moxhay*:

- *The covenant must be negative or restrictive in nature*: the burden of a positive covenant cannot run. A positive covenant requires expenditure of money or labour: for example, a covenant to keep a property in good repair is positive. The test is one of substance – it does not matter how the covenant is worded, so a covenant not to permit a property to fall into disrepair is also positive.

- *The covenantee must at the time the covenant is made and afterwards own the land which benefits from the covenant.* (*London CC v Allen* [1914]); (*Dano Ltd v Earl Cadogen* [2003]).

- *The covenant must touch and concern the dominant land.*

- *It must be the common intention of the parties that the burden of the covenant shall run with the land of the covenantor*: this will usually be implied, unless a contrary intention is expressed, by virtue of s 79 of the LPA 1925.

> ### TULK v MOXHAY [1848]
>
> **The burden of a covenant may run in equity if the purchaser has notice of the covenant.**
>
> Facts
>
> The claimant sold land in Leicester Square to the covenantor who covenanted to keep the land in an open state. The covenantor later sold the land to the defendant who was aware of the covenant. The defendant attempted to build on the land and the court had to determine whether the covenant was enforceable.
>
> Held
>
> The court held that the covenant was binding because the defendant had notice of it.

THE PROBLEM OF POSITIVE COVENANTS

Because of the rules in *Austerberry* and *Tulk v Moxhay* [1848], the burden of a positive covenant cannot run with freehold land.

Some properties, however, require enforceable positive obligations for the management and maintenance of the land. For example, the occupiers of a block of flats need to ensure that the common parts (landings, stairways, lifts, etc) are maintained. For this reason, most flats have tended to be leasehold, so that a covenant to maintain the common parts can be enforced as a leasehold covenant.

A number of methods of enforcing positive covenants with freehold land have been tried with varying degrees of success:

- Identical covenants may be taken by each successive purchaser, thereby forming a chain of indemnity. The chain can be broken, however.

- The doctrine of mutual benefit and burden may apply (*Halsall v Brizell* [1957]). The benefit must be related to the burden (*Rhone v Stephens*

FREEHOLD COVENANTS

[1994]) and the burden will only be enforced if the assignee chooses to exercise the benefit (*Thamesmead Town Ltd v Allotey* [1998]).

- Section 79 of the LPA 1925 is unlikely to be useful, as it does not annex the burden of a covenant to the land (*Tophams v Earl of Sefton* [1967]; *Rhone v Stephens* [1994]).

- A long lease may be granted, which is then enlarged to a fee simple (s 153(1) of the LPA 1925).

- An estate rentcharge may be created for the maintenance of the property (s 2(3)(c) of the Rentcharges Act 1977).

- A right of entry may be reserved (*Shiloh Spinners Ltd v Harding* [1973]).

- Tenants of flats may form a management company to be the landlord. The company is then able to enforce positive obligations under the lease.

- New developments may be subject to the Commonhold and Leasehold Reform Act 2002. In a commonhold scheme, the landowners (unit holders) hold a freehold estate in commonhold land. This is a freehold together with an unseverable share in a commonhold association (a company formed to own the common parts and manage the commonhold land). The commonhold association is able to enforce positive obligations against the unit holders. Existing developments may be converted to a commonhold scheme, but only if all parties agree to the change.

▶ HALSALL v BRIZELL [1957]

Under an ancient rule of law, 'a man cannot take the benefit under a deed without subscribing to the obligations thereunder'.

Facts

In 1851 the original owners of sea-front properties covenanted to pay for the maintenance of sewers, a road, a sea wall, and a promenade. The covenants were expressed to be for themselves, their heirs, executors and assigns. In 1950 the executors of one of the subsequent owners refused to comply with the terms of the covenants. They argued that, as the covenants were positive in nature they were incapable of running with the land.

> **Held**
> The court found that if the occupiers wished to benefit from the covenants by using the road and sewers they must also be bound by the burden.

DISCHARGE AND MODIFICATION OF COVENANTS

By unity of seisin: if both plots of land come into common ownership, the covenant cannot be enforced.

By release: the covenantee may release the covenantor by deed, or release may be implied from the facts. For example, if the character of the neighbourhood has changed so as to make the covenant worthless, or if the covenantee has acquiesced in open breaches, it may be held that the covenantee has impliedly released the covenantor from the obligation, or that he has abandoned the covenant.

By the Lands Tribunal: s 84(1) of the LPA 1925 gives the Lands Tribunal powers to modify or discharge covenants in such circumstances as obsolescence.

Remedies for breach of covenant

- *Common law damages*: available when the original covenantee sues the original covenantor or when the assignee of the covenantee sues the original covenantor (*Surrey CC v Bredero Homes Ltd* [1993]).
- *Interlocutory injunction.*
- *Final injunction.*
- *Equitable damages – damages in lieu of an injunction under s 50 of the Supreme Court Act 1981*: for example, in *Wrotham Park Estate Ltd v Parkside Homes Ltd* [1974], damages in lieu of an injunction were awarded because to order demolition of a housing estate, which had been built in breach of covenant, would be a waste of good housing.

You should now be confident that you would be able to tick all the boxes on the checklist at the beginning of this chapter. To check your knowledge of Freehold covenants why not visit the companion website and take the Multiple Choice Question test. Check your understanding of the terms and vocabulary used in this chapter with the flashcard glossary.

11

Putting it into practice...

PUTTING IT INTO PRACTICE . . .

Now that you've mastered the basics, you will want to put it all into practice. The Routledge Questions and Answers series provides an ideal opportunity for you to apply your understanding and knowledge of the law and to hone your essay-writing technique.

We've included one exam-style essay question, which replicates the type of question posed in the Routledge Questions and Answers series to give you some essential exam practice. The Q&A includes a fully worked model answer to help you recognise what examiners might look for in your answer.

QUESTION 1

General Greatcliff has for many years owned a large sixteenth-century mansion, Greatcliff Heights ('the property'), on the North East coast. The property has a delightful aspect overlooking a beautiful lake. Unfortunately for the General, a local builder, Jim Jones, became interested in the strip of land between the property and the lake on which he was proposing to build a theme park. A neighbouring guest house owner, Bill Proffit, was furious at the prospect of losing his lake view, and the anticipated surge of tourists that such a project would attract to the local area. He called a meeting of the General and all local hotel and guest house owners. At this meeting, it was decided that the owners of the properties which would be affected by the proposed construction would purchase the strip of land between them. The land was accordingly purchased by Bill, Carrie, Dorothy, Eric, Fred and the General. Bill insisted that the names were put in that order on the conveyance, to reflect the business owners first.

A few years ago, Fred discovered that his hotel was haunted, and he sold both his hotel and his share in the strip of land to a Construct-X company, who wished to sell the strip to Jim Jones so that they could develop the theme park together. Then, Carrie argued with Bill and sold her hotel and her share in the strip of land to Construct-X. Eric died in a car accident last year, and his executors would like to sell the strip of land to Construct-X in order to raise money for his estate. Dorothy too has received a good offer from Construct-X and wants to sell the strip of land. Carrie is indifferent as she sold her equitable interest some time ago. Bill, who is adamant that the strip of land should not be sold, is seriously ill with an incurable tropical fever.

QUESTION 1

Advise the General as to whether Construct-X will be able to sell the strip of land to Jim Jones.

Answer

Since 1 January 1997, it has been possible to create only one type of trust of land. Section 1 of the Trusts of Land and Appointment of Trustees Act 1996 (TOLATA) provides that 'trust of land' means ... any trust which consists of or includes land...

Whenever land is conveyed to two or more persons, a statutory trust will come into existence (ss 34–36 of the Law of Property Act 1925) (LPA). If the title of land is registered, the registrar is obliged to enter a restriction on the register if he registers two or more persons as the proprietors of a registered estate (s 44 Land Registration Act 2002) (LRA).

The trustees hold the legal estate; they are the legal owners. The names of the trustees will be on the conveyance or, if title to the land is registered, the trustees will be registered at the Land Registry as the proprietors. The trustees do not own the land absolutely: they have a duty to administer the trust for the beneficiaries. In many cases of co-ownership, the trustees and beneficiaries are the same persons.

There must not be more than four trustees (s 34(2) LPA 1925 and s 34(2) Trustees Act 1925 (TA). If land is conveyed to more than four people and the trustees have not been nominated, the first four named will be the trustees.

In the scenario, there are six persons involved. The trustees have been nominated and are Bill, Carrie, Dorothy and Eric.

The legal estate is **always** held as a joint tenancy, with a right of survivorship. It can **never** be severed to form a tenancy in common (s 1(6) and s 36(2) LPA 1925).

The trustees have all the powers of an absolute owner (s 6(1) TOLATA 1996). In exercising their functions, trustees must, so far as practicable, consult all of the beneficiaries who are of full age and beneficially entitled to an interest in possession of the land. They should, so far as consistent with the general interest of the trust, give effect to the wishes of the majority (according to the value of their combined interests (s 11 TOLATA 1996)).

PUTTING IT INTO PRACTICE . . .

Unlike the legal estate, which must be held as a joint tenancy, a beneficial interest may be held as a tenancy in common (undivided share). Each beneficial tenant in common has his own share of the property and the right of survivorship will not apply. A tenant in common may leave his share to somebody by will, or it will devolve according to the rules of intestacy in the absence of a will. A tenant in common may also sell or give away his share whilst he is still alive. If he does so, he will remain a trustee until he dies or retires from office.

A joint tenancy is characterised by the four unities (*A G Securities v Vaughan* [1990]). If any of the unities are absent, there cannot be a joint tenancy and the interest will be a tenancy in common. The four unities are possession, interest, time and title. A joint tenancy can be severed by a variety of processes.

Additionally a tenancy in common can be created by using words of severance, for example, 'equally' or to be divided between. A tenancy in common will also be presumed where commercial partners acquire a property together (*Lake v Craddock* [1955]), or when purchasers contribute in unequal shares (*Bull v Bull* [1955]), for business tenants (*Malayan Credit Ltd v Jack Chia-MPH Ltd* [1986]), or mortgagees between themselves (*Petty Skyward* [1631]). In the scenario, B, C, D and E are trustees and will hold the legal title as Joint Tenants (s 1(6) and s 36(2) LPA 1925).

Although the unities appear to be fulfilled, equity will favour a tenancy in common because the parties are commercial partners. Most are hotel or guest house owners and are purchasing the land with a view to protecting their businesses.

Since the purchase, several events have occurred, and it is necessary to analyse them in chronological order, to advise whether or not the strip of land can be sold.

Upon finding out that his hotel was haunted, Fred sold both his hotel and his share in the strip to a Construct-X company. We need to assess how this affected the legal and equitable ownership of the land. Fred was not a trustee, so the legal estate will remain unaffected; B, C, D and E remain as trustees. Since the equitable ownership was a tenancy in common for all of the parties, Fred was at liberty to sell his equitable share to Construct-X, and they will now hold a 1/6 share of the land as an equitable tenant in common. Construct-X will not hold a legal interest.

QUESTION 1

The next event that occurred was when Carrie sold her share to Construct-X. Carrie, as a trustee, had a legal interest as a Joint Tenant in the land. This cannot be severed, thus Carrie will remain a trustee until she either dies, or retires her position. Construct-X will not replace her as a trustee. Construct-X will however acquire Carrie's equitable share in the strip of land and its beneficial ownership will increase to 2/6 (or 1/3) of the equitable interest.

Last year Eric died in a car accident. This will affect the legal estate, as Eric was a trustee and held a legal interest as a Joint Tenant. When a Joint Tenant dies, the rule of survivorship will operate, and Eric's legal interest will pass to B, C, and D, who will now be Joint Tenants of the whole legal estate. We are not aware of the content of Eric's will, thus Eric's equitable interest of 1/6 will pass to the executors of his estate to dispose of either by the instructions in his will, or through the rules of intestacy.

At this juncture, it would be pertinent to consider the constitution of the legal and equitable estates. B, C and D are the legal owners; the trustees. The beneficial owners all hold their interests as tenants in common, as follows: Construct-X own 1/3 of the equitable interest, Bill owns 1/6, Dorothy owns 1/6, Eric's executors own 1/6 and the General owns 1/6.

The current situation with the trustees is that both Eric's executors and Dorothy want the strip of land to be sold. Carrie could be persuaded as she has no real interest either way, but Bill does not want to sell.

The current situation with the beneficiaries is that both Eric's executors and Dorothy want the strip of land to be sold, and Carrie could be persuaded. Construct-X want to sell – they have a 1/3 interest. It is unlikely that the General would want the land to be sold when we consider his reasons for the purchase.

Under s 6(1) TOLATA, the trustees have the power of sale, but their decision upon whether to sell is not unanimous here, as Bill is unwilling. In addition under s 11 TOLATA, the trustees must 'so far as practicable' consult the beneficiaries of full age and, 'so far as consistent with the general interest of the trust' give effect to their wishes. Here a decision to sell would be consistent with the majority's wishes – Construct-X, Dorothy and Eric's executors have 4/6 between them. Construct-X has no legal interest in the land, so do not have any power under s 6 TOLATA.

PUTTING IT INTO PRACTICE...

Under a trust of land, the power to sell or postpone sale exists. There is no duty to sell. In the current situation, only two out of the three trustees wish to sell. This will pose a problem, as all names must appear on the conveyance and receipt of monies.

Where a dispute arises in the sale of trust property, s 14 of TOLATA provides a mechanism for any person interested (trustee, beneficiary, mortgagee) to apply to the court for an order of sale, or to prevent a sale. The court can, under s 14, make 'such order as the court thinks fit'. Thus any of the parties requiring a sale could apply to the court under s 14 TOLATA. Upon receipt of such a request, the court will want to know whether s 11 has been complied with. We are aware that the majority of beneficial owners wish to sell. However, the General and Bill can object under ss 14 and 15 (1)(a) & (b) on the grounds that the original purpose of the trust still exists – i.e., the land is being held to stop Jim Jones from developing it. This scenario is similar to the facts of *Re Buchanan-Wollaston's Conveyance* [1939]. The court will decide whether the purpose of the trust has dissolved but must also take on board the views of the majority of the beneficiaries. If the precedent is followed in *Re Buchanan-Wollaston's Conveyance* [1939], the court may refuse to order a sale of the land.

It also appears that Bill's recovery is unlikely. Bill is the only trustee preventing the sale. If Bill died, the remaining two trustees could then sell the land (s 6 TOLATA). The interests of the beneficiaries would be overreached on sale provided that the capital money is paid to, and a receipt obtained from the trustees, being at least two in number. If the General applied to the court under s 14 TOLATA, to prevent the sale, his argument may not find favour, as he would be the only remaining person who wished to prevent a sale. In this instance, the court may no longer be convinced that the purpose of the trust still exists.

Each Routledge Q&A contains 50 essay and problem-based questions on topics commonly found on exam papers, complete with answer plans and fully worked model answers. For further examination practice, visit the Routledge website or your local bookstore today!

ROUTLEDGE LAWCARDS

are your complete, up-to-date pocket-sized guides to key examinable areas of the undergraduate law curriculum and the CPE/GDL.

New editions of all titles in the series are publishing in February 2010.

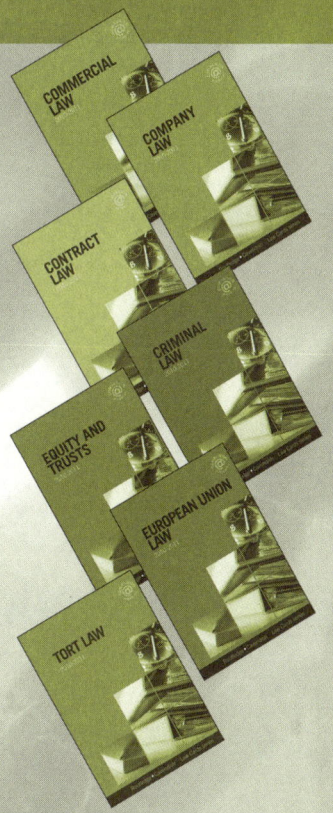

Commercial Law 2010-2011
Company Law 2010-2011
Constitutional & Administrative Law 2010-2011
Contract Law 2010-2011
Criminal Law 2010-2011
Employment Law 2010-2011
English Legal System 2010-2011
European Union Law 2010-2011
Evidence 2010-2011
Family Law 2010-2011
Human Rights Law 2010-2011
Intellectual Property Law 2010-2011
Jurisprudence 2010-2011
Land Law 2010-2011
Tort Law 2010-2011
Equity & Trusts 2010-2011

For a full listing, visit:
www.routledgelaw.com/revisionaids.asp

Routledge
Taylor & Francis Group

ROUTLEDGE Q&A SERIES

Each Routledge Q&A contains 50 questions on topics commonly found on exam papers, with comprehensive suggested answers. The titles are written by lecturers who are also examiners, so the student gains an important insight into exactly what examiners are looking for in an answer. This makes them excellent revision and practice guides.

Titles in the series include:
Business Law
Civil Liberties & Human Rights
Company Law
Commercial Law
Constitutional & Administrative Law
Contract Law
Criminal Law
Employment Law
English Legal System
Equity & Trusts
European Union Law
Evidence
Family Law
Intellectual Property Law
Jurisprudence
Land Law
Torts

For a full listing, visit:
www.routledgelaw.com/revisionaids.asp

Routledge
Taylor & Francis Group